A FIELD GUIDE TO

TEQUILA

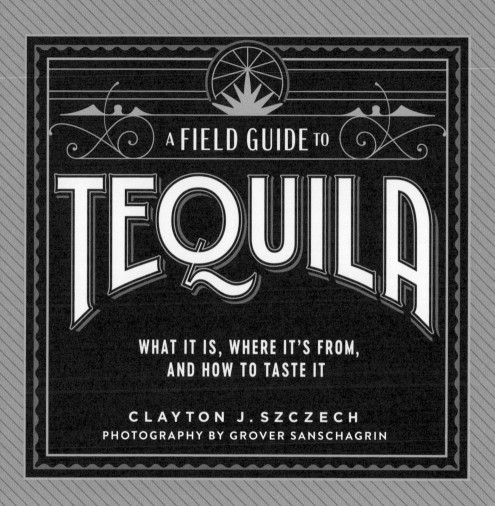

A FIELD GUIDE TO

TEQUILA

WHAT IT IS, WHERE IT'S FROM, AND HOW TO TASTE IT

CLAYTON J. SZCZECH
PHOTOGRAPHY BY GROVER SANSCHAGRIN

ARTISAN | NEW YORK

Photographs copyright © 2023 by Grover Sanschagrin except page 176: pacoadame/
Shutterstock.com; and page 207: Top Shelf International
Author photograph by Tony Sams
Illustrations by Holly Wales, except page 24: *The Book of the Life of the Ancient Mexicans
(Codex Magliabechiano)*, Biblioteca Nazionale Centrale di Firenze, Berkeley, CA: University of
California, 1903, courtesy of Special Collections, J. Willard Marriott Library, The University
of Utah; and page 184 (top to bottom): LDarin/Shutterstock.com, Maksym
Drozd / Shutterstock.com, Chanawin Tepprasitsakda / Shutterstock.com, Pogorelova
Olga / Shutterstock.com

Library of Congress Cataloging-in-Publication Data
Names: Szczech, Clayton J., author. | Sanschagrin, Grover, photographer.
Title: A field guide to tequila / Clayton J. Szczech;
photography by Grover Sanschagrin.
Description: New York, NY : Artisan, [2023] |
Includes bibliographical references and index.
Identifiers: LCCN 2023001033 | ISBN 9781648291487 (hardback)
Subjects: LCSH: Tequila.
Classification: LCC TP607.T46 S93 2023 | DDC 663/.5—dc23/eng/20230201
LC record available at https://lccn.loc.gov/2023001033

Design by Lisa Hollander
Cover design by Suet Chong
Cover illustration by Abraham Lule

Artisan books are available at special discounts when purchased in bulk
for premiums and sales promotions as well as for fundraising or educational use.
Special editions or book excerpts can also be created to specification.
For details, please contact special.markets@hbgusa.com.

The publisher is not responsible for websites (or their content)
that are not owned by the publisher.

The Hachette Speakers Bureau provides a wide range of authors
for speaking events. To find out more, go to
hachettespeakersbureau.com or email HachetteSpeakers@hbgusa.com.

Published by Artisan,
an imprint of Workman Publishing Co., Inc.,
a subsidiary of Hachette Book Group, Inc.
1290 Avenue of the Americas
New York, NY 10104
artisanbooks.com

Printed in China on responsibly sourced paper

First printing, September 2023

10 9 8 7 6 5 4 3 2 1

Dedicated to the people of Jalisco
and to the beloved memories of Tomás Estes,
José Luís González Partida, Javier Delgado Corona,
and Berta Torres Mireles

CONTENTS

PREFACE

I know some of my best friends thanks to tequila. The spirit has provided me with a meaningful and rewarding career. It has facilitated my acceptance into worlds far beyond the one I was born into. I'm recognized as a passionate advocate for tequila as one of the world's finest spirits, a drink that represents more than four centuries of Mexican cultural legacy. I am deeply grateful to tequila. But it wasn't always like this.

Like many people, I got off on the wrong foot with tequila. My youthful ignorance, inexperience, and exuberance led to overindulgence and a vow to steer clear of Mexico's national drink forever. It's a common story, and one that may have ended there had I not gone to a dear friend's wedding in Texas en route to moving to Mexico to teach high school in 2006.

I first politely declined a glass of tequila, alluding to my past experiences. My friend's brother kindly but firmly reminded me that I was in San Antonio, at a Mexican American wedding, and I was also about to move to Mexico. Given the circumstances, there was no way I was going to refuse to enjoy tequila with them—*caray*! I yielded, of course. That night I discovered that good tequila treats the drinker with exactly as much respect as it is given and that there's just something about a tequila buzz that seems brighter and happier than other experiences. After a weekend of responsibly imbibing quality tequila in the company of friends old and new, I settled in Mexico with a fresh curiosity about the spirit.

I now appreciated tequila's traditional role of cementing social bonds and marking momentous life occasions. With a new attitude of reverence, I began to slowly build a small tequila collection. I wondered how some of it could be so delicious and some of it so terrible. I started searching for answers in the public library, where I read every Spanish-language text on tequila I could find, and in an online tequila forum, where I found a community of aficionados who were eager to help me learn.

Nearly a year later, I knew more about tequila than most people, but it was all abstract knowledge. It was hard for me to imagine what tequila production was like in real life—especially the stuff about agaves. This bizarre-looking plant that took years to grow and was sacrificed to make tequila seemed like something out of a science fiction novel. I had to go and see it for myself.

The town of Tequila, with its epic volcano and expansive blue agave fields, was unlike any place I had ever been. It captivated me, and the local people were friendly and receptive to my barrage of questions about how tequila was made and how it fit into their lives. I began to form friendships in Tequila that have lasted to this day. I was moved by my experience, and I wanted my old friends to meet my new friends in Tequila. In fact, I wanted to share this experience with anyone who was curious about where tequila came from. I was still young and impulsive enough that I decided to start a tour company that would bring people to Jalisco for an immersive experience in tequila culture, much like the one I had enjoyed myself. I had zero business experience and no real idea of what I was doing, but I had the energy and zeal of a new convert. And the people of Tequila were kind, generous with their time, and proud to share their way of life with the small groups I began bringing down in 2009.

To become a better guide, I undertook a serious study of all aspects of tequila from the ground up. I spent days in the fields with farmers, laborers, and botanists, in distilleries with *tequileros*, workers, and engineers, in laboratories with chemists, and in tasting rooms, bars, and cantinas with anyone with a story to tell. Since I first set foot in Mexico in 1995, I had learned again and again that an outsider's sincere and respectful interest in the culture means a lot to people. Even so, I was routinely humbled by the time, insight, and sincerity offered to me by everyone: old-timers on the plaza, bottling-line workers, anxious first-time agave growers, and the industry's brightest stars.

Those folks taught me a lot about tequila. My tour business started doing well enough that I could quit my job and make tequila my full-time gig. Soon, I was leading tours in Jalisco nine months of the year and spending summers hosting tastings, judging competitions, and speaking at tequila festivals. I eventually began consulting and training tequila bar workforces throughout the United States. I continued to learn as I taught, seeking out maestros throughout the industry and in academia, earning various certifications and continuing to read absolutely everything tequila-related that I could get my hands on.

My clients have been hard-core aficionados, tequila-skeptical vacationers, business owners, bartenders, trade associations, journalists, and even a Canadian bank. A common question everyone asks me is, "Can you recommend a good tequila book?" I've read them all, but most of the best sources are available only in Spanish. There are excellent academic books written in English, but they are not entirely accessible nor are they exactly what people are looking for. A few of my favorite books are classics, but they are years out of date and many are out of print. Tequila has grown and evolved quite a lot even in the short amount of time I have known it, and a lot of the information out there is incorrect, incomplete, biased, or hard to find. My best recommendation has been to amass a collection of a dozen or more books and to focus on the strongest parts of each one to gain a better understanding of tequila. But there is no single book that I can hand to someone and say, "Start here."

You can see where this is going. At some point, I realized that no one else was going to write that book, and that I was well suited to do it.

I had a pile of notebooks going back to my very first trip to Tequila and extensive contacts throughout the region that I could tap for insight, perspective, and fact-checking. As a tour guide and researcher without financial ties to any tequila brand, I had enjoyed years of access to any tequila distillery I had cared to visit. So, my perspective on tequila is broader, deeper, and possibly even more objective than most.

While I've managed to become fairly erudite when it comes to tequila, I'm no snob, and it has always been my goal to teach by demystifying and speaking as plainly as possible. That has also been my goal in writing this book. *A Field Guide to Tequila* contains an awful lot of information about tequila—historical, legal, technical, and gustatory. I think you will find most of your questions about tequila answered in its pages. What you won't find is judgment about your personal relationship with tequila. We all start somewhere, and no one starting point is better than any other. My own tequila journey would never have begun were it not for the camaraderie of my hosts at that wedding and the open-mindedness of my friends in Jalisco. I wrote this book in that spirit of sharing.

Whether you're a pinkies-up, slow-sipping aficionado, a happy-hour margarita imbiber, a shots-on-the-beach type, or merely tequila-curious, this book should add to, enhance, and deepen whatever relationship you currently have with tequila. I hope it will bring you even a fraction of the enjoyment that tequila has brought into my own life.

INTRODUCTION

These days, it seems like everyone drinks tequila; or at least, most people drink tequila, and everyone has an opinion about it. Some swear tequila is healthy and that the good stuff can't cause hangovers. Others are still telling that one story about when they overdid it on spring break and swore off tequila for good. Passionate bartenders enthuse about craft, quality, and tradition, while sun-wizened snowbird retirees bemoan how expensive tequila has become.

One thing is certain: At no point in history have more people been drinking tequila. In 2021, amid a pandemic, an unprecedented 527 million liters (139 million gallons) of tequila were produced. Consumers, primarily in the United States and Mexico, sipped and mixed it all up to the tune of more than $8 billion. A 2022 beverage industry report projected that tequila (along with the tiny mezcal category) would overtake American whiskey sales in the United States that same year and would surpass vodka by 2023. Tequila is more popular than it has ever been, and it appears that its popularity will only increase.

But tequila enthusiasts outside of Mexico still know surprisingly little about the beverage: where it's from, how it's made, and why flavor profiles within the tequila category vary so widely. And few are aware that the industry's very success has created conditions that threaten its sustainability.

The agave plant's peculiar life cycle, Mexico's rugged geography and turbulent history, and enduring apprehensions about tequila have all contributed to the spirit's dramatic biography. The ups, downs, and zigzags of tequila's history are a fascinating part of how it became what it is today.

About 400 years ago, a distilling tradition was born in the Tequila-Amatitán Valley, in what is now western Mexico. This distillation of local wild agave plants was one of several regional mezcal traditions to crop up in the early seventeenth century. Eventually, rural landowners appropriated this collective Indigenous craft as a source of private wealth. Those *hacendados* would become some of independent Mexico's first capitalists, and with the advent of the railroad and glass bottles, "tequila" began to distinguish itself as a commodity apart from other mezcals approximately 150 years ago. But in the lean years between the Mexican Revolution (1910–1921) and the Second World War, tequila nearly vanished, only to begin a slow but steady recovery in the second half of the twentieth century.

It's difficult to truly comprehend how small the industry had become in the middle part of the twentieth century. In 1972, for example, there were only about thirty active tequila distilleries (compared to around 140 in 2023).

US demand for tequila and tequila cocktails in the 1970s, 1980s, and 1990s created a steadily increasing boom that made tequila one of a few truly global spirits. While the English-speaking world has come a long way from eye-rolling puns ("te-kill-ya") and references to "cactus juice," sophistication in consumption has far outpaced depth of understanding of tequila.

A Field Guide to Tequila is an attempt to change that. It's for anyone who is at all interested in tequila: what it is, where it is from, how it is made, how to select and taste it, how to continue learning more about it, and how to be a more ethical tequila consumer. This book was designed to educate and engage readers who know nothing about tequila, to serve as a reference for seasoned connoisseurs, and to enhance the knowledge of everyone in between.

CHAPTER 1

DEFINING TEQUILA

WHAT IT IS AND WHERE IT'S FROM

WHAT IS TEQUILA?

Tequila is a Mexican liquor distilled from the fermented juice of the cooked blue agave plant. Most Mexican agave spirits are known as *mezcales*, and tequila was born as a regional mezcal called *"vino mezcal de Tequila."* In the early days of Spanish colonization (beginning in 1519), the word "vino"—"wine"—was used to refer to any alcoholic beverage, including distilled spirits. This is still the case today in some parts of Mexico. The word "mezcal" referred to the agave plant itself and still does in certain Mexican rural areas. A distilled "wine from the mezcal plant," what we would now call a mezcal, was being produced in the Tequila-Amatitán Valley by 1640. As the region's mezcal production grew into an industry and garnered wider recognition, the spirit came to be known simply as "tequila."

The word "mezcal" comes from the words for "cooked agave" in the indigenous Nahuatl language, and it became the colloquial name for all Mexican agave spirits. "Tequila" is the Hispanicized rendering of *tequitlan*, meaning "place of work" or "place of tribute." This was the name of the now-dormant volcano that dominates the landscape of the Tequila Valley. For centuries before the Spanish invasion, local inhabitants collected obsidian from around the volcano and worked it into tools, weapons, and adornments. The volcano's name would eventually

Opposite page: Fernando González, owner of Tequila Siete Leguas (page 146), collects a sample during distillation.

be taken on by the village at its foot, the entire valley, and the beverage that made the region famous.

These days, tequila is defined by specific laws and regulations. These rules prescribe the "where," "what," and "how" of tequila. A beverage that does not check off all three boxes cannot be sold as tequila. More formally, we can say that tequila is a distilled spirit made from a single varietal of agave ("the what"), in specific parts of Mexico ("the where"), according to rules established by the Mexican government, as interpreted and enforced by the Tequila Regulatory Council ("the how").

TEQUILA HISTORY
FROM THE SPANISH CONQUEST TO EARLY EXPORTS

1519 The Spanish invasion begins. Fermented alcoholic beverages have long been consumed throughout Mesoamerica. While there is no widespread Indigenous distillation, it is possible that a few communities are already distilling spirits.

1530 The Spanish conquer what is now the municipality of Tequila, and Guadalajara is established twelve years later. Colonial authorities officially prohibit Indigenous alcohol consumption, seeing it as an impediment to religious conversion and labor productivity.

1560s TO 1616 The Spanish open a trade route between their Asian and American colonies, bringing ships laden with Filipino migrants, servants, and goods into Nueva Galicia (which includes the modern-day state of Jalisco). Filipinos introduce wooden stills, which they use to turn fermented coco palm sap into a spirit called *vino de cocos*. After 1616, this Asian distilling tradition is adopted by Indigenous and rural communities throughout Nueva Galicia.

1620s TO 1640s Distillation of cooked agave begins in the Valley of Tequila. The Indigenous community in the Tecuane canyon (now within the municipality of Amatitán) harvests wild *mezcal* (agave), cooks it underground, ferments it in stone pits, and likely distills it with wood and copper "Filipino-style" stills. This spirit becomes known as *vino mezcal*.

1637 ᵀᴼ 1700s In an effort to protect the profits of winemakers, the Spanish introduce various prohibitions on alcohol production. These regulations are short-lived as they are difficult to enforce and reduce tax revenue for the Crown. Taxes on vino mezcal will eventually fund construction of the port of San Blas, and both Guadalajara's municipal water system and its iconic Palacio de Gobierno.

1795 King Carlos II grants José María Guadalupe de Cuervo y Montaño permission to produce vino mezcal commercially, although Cuervo has been distilling since 1758. There are already a handful of landowners producing vino mezcal on their haciendas, as well as small producers operating ad hoc stills in the canyons, staying one step ahead of the tax collector.

1810 ᵀᴼ 1860s Tequila production is severely disrupted by Mexico's War of Independence (1810–1821). The war increases tequila demand and closes the port of Acapulco, temporarily making San Blas (much closer to the Tequila Valley) Mexico's most important Pacific port. This facilitates the development of an export market for vino mezcal de Tequila. By the middle of the nineteenth century, writers begin referring to the regional mezcal as simply "tequila." But the "mezcal de" prefix will remain on labels for another century.

AGAVES AND HUMANS
A LOVE STORY

Agaves are kind of a big deal. Actually, they are a really big deal. The agave's importance to the development of Mesoamerican civilization is arguably without equal in the plant world. This group of succulents had evolved for approximately 14 million years before humans arrived in America, perfectly adapting to harsh, dry conditions. When the Spanish invaded Mexico in 1519, Indigenous people had been using agaves for food, shelter, and clothing for more than 10,000 years. Not surprisingly, they revered the plant as sacred. The Spanish immediately realized the agave's cultural and material importance, calling it "the tree of wonders." When agaves arrived in Europe as exotic samples of New World flora, they quickly became trendy additions to private and public gardens throughout the continent. European naturalists studiously sketched, measured, and classified agaves, which they erroneously associated with African aloes. In 1753, when Swedish botanist Carl Linnaeus devised the taxonomic system used to classify all living things, he personally christened these succulent American plants "agave," from the ancient Greek for "noble" or "admirable." It is clear why agaves were important to Indigenous Mexicans, but why were outsiders so immediately drawn to and fascinated by these plants?

For one thing, it was impossible to ignore the agave's uniquely imposing physical appearance. Its swordlike *pencas*, or leaves, jut into the sky, are bordered by thorns, and come to a point in fang-like spines that can pierce thick clothing and leather boots. They seem to grow everywhere in Mexico, from arid deserts to pine forests, taking over valley floors and clinging desperately to rocky cliffsides. When in bloom, they are like nothing else on the planet. In Mexico's diverse and challenging geography, agaves are an obvious symbol of survival in the face of adversity.

These survivors helped human beings weather the same harsh environments, and an evolutionary symbiosis between agaves and *Homo sapiens* developed. As a primary source of caloric energy and nutrients, agaves facilitated human migration and settlement throughout Mexico. Cooked and split into small pieces, agave could be carried as sustenance on long journeys. On those same journeys, living agaves could be tapped for their nutritious sap when there was no fresh water. That sap contains protein and vitamins that are crucial for human survival. Fibrous agave species were eventually turned into clothing, shoes, and bandages. Entire homes were made from different agave parts: the long woody flower stalks served as lumber for walls and roofs, which were thatched with agave leaves and held together by agave-fiber rope. The sap of various agave species was used to make soap, medicines, vinegar, and, eventually, the fermented alcoholic beverage *pulque* (see The Goddess Mayahuel and Pulque, page 24). When agaves died and dried out, they were used as fuel for warmth and cooking. In the Aztec Empire, the agave's spines were used for ritual piercings and to torture captured enemies.

The agave's many uses inspired migratory communities to transport the plant with them, which increased its natural range even more, as they selected certain species for food and drink, others for fiber and building materials, others for soap, medicine, and so on. In this way, humans and agaves evolved together for thousands of years.

Europeans were astounded not only by the agave's unique physical characteristics and usefulness, but also by the plant's facility for reproduction. Centuries later, our scientific understanding of agaves has done nothing to diminish the plants' grandeur. The agave's life cycle is a chain of dramatic and breathtaking events. Growing agaves clone themselves dozens of times, while living off sunlight, minerals in the soil, and sparse annual rainfall. After a few years of aggressively hoarding solar energy in the form of complex carbohydrate chains, they propel all of that energy and matter upward in the form of a spectacular flower stalk. Once they've exhausted all their stored energy in this Herculean reproductive effort, they die heroically, enriching the soil that will give rise to a new generation of agave.

THE GODDESS
MAYAHUEL AND PULQUE

The genus of agaves provided for many basic needs of Mesoamerican peoples. Among its uses, several large agave species were tapped to extract their nutritious sap, which was consumed fresh as *aguamiel* ("honey-water") or fermented into *pulque*.

Above: Painting of the goddess Mayahuel, dated from sometime between 1529 and 1553. Source: *The Book of the Life of the Ancient Mexicans (Codex Magliabechiano).*
Opposite page: Statue of the modernized Mayahuel in Tequila, Jalisco.

Pulque is often mistakenly believed to be a precursor of tequila, but they are distinct traditions. Pulque is made from various agave species in many parts of Mexico. The central highlands encompassing the states of Mexico, Puebla, Tlaxcala, and Hidalgo are the epicenter of pulque production.

To make tequila, agave must be cooked to produce fermentable sugar. Pulque, however, is fermented from the raw sap of living agaves. Slow bacterial fermentation turns the agave's sweet aguamiel into somewhat milky pulque, which contains a plethora of nutrients and has an alcohol by volume (ABV) of between 4% and 5%.

Aztec priests used pulque for ritual purposes, and harshly punished drunkenness among commoners. Agave was eventually deified as the goddess Mayahuel. In myth, Mayahuel eloped with the powerful god Quetzalcoatl and was turned into an agave as punishment. As a fertility goddess, Mayahuel was well represented on earth by the prolific agaves, which produce phallic *quiotes* (flower stalks), millions of seeds, and scores of *hijuelos* (clones). Mayahuel's 400 breasts produced pulque to nurse her 400 rabbit children. These rabbit children represented the 400 types, or levels, of inebriation.

Mayahuel is far older than distillation and tequila. But the enterprising Francisco Javier Sauza (see page 140) would successfully appropriate her as a "tequila goddess" in the 1960s. The fierce, Indigenous, centenary-breasted deity wasn't exactly on-brand for Sauza, who was determined to make tequila acceptable to skeptical *gringos*. So, in Sauza's marketing materials, he turned her into a demure European-featured beauty, modeled after Sophia Loren!

BASIC AGAVE BIOLOGY

Agaves are a genus of succulent plants that grow in arid and semi-arid environments. There are more than 200 species of agave, and around 70% are endemic to Mexico.

Agaves are not cacti. In fact, they are more closely related to lilies and onions. Nevertheless, parallel evolution in the same extreme environments resulted in shared adaptive strategies. Agaves and cacti are both succulents: They hoard water beneath a tough, waxy skin. Both rely on long, sharp thorns and spines to deter would-be animal predators. Most importantly, both have evolved what is called "CAM metabolism," meaning that they open their pores to "breathe" only at night.

In temperate zones, plants open their pores, or stomata, during the day, exchanging oxygen for carbon dioxide. They simultaneously absorb solar energy, which fuels growth by converting CO_2 and water into carbohydrates. In a desert, this kind of daytime respiration would completely dehydrate a plant. Instead, agaves act as a solar-powered battery during the day, storing energy until night, when they open their stomata and "breathe." It seems appropriate that the plants that fuel so many late-night human revelries are themselves most active in the small hours.

Opposite page: Blue agaves grow among wildflowers in the Tequila Valley.

AGAVE REPRODUCTION

Agaves are survivors and profligate reproducers. Like all organisms, they are "programmed" by nature to pass along as much of their genetic material as possible to future generations. Agaves' success in the natural selection game is in large part due to their adaptability and

ASEXUAL REPRODUCTION BY RHIZOME

Many species of agave will produce clones early in their life cycle. The adult plant generates underground rhizomes or "runners" that emerge nearby as baby agaves, which are called "hijuelos" and are exact genetic copies of the parent plant. While it's common to refer to the hijuelo-producing agave as the "mother plant," we now know that the blue agave is hermaphroditic: Every plant has both male and female sex chromosomes.

SEXUAL REPRODUCTION

Left to its own devices, a healthy agave will produce a quiote, or flower stalk, as it nears the end of its life cycle. All the energy the agave has absorbed from the sun and hoarded in the form of carbohydrates produces the quiote in a dramatic burst of growth—about an inch a day! The quiote produces

multiple methods of reproduction. Agaves as a genus can naturally reproduce in at least three different ways: by rhizome, sexually, and by bulbil.

flowers, which attract pollinators such as bats, which distribute pollen among agave flowers as they feed on the nectar. Pollinated flowers will produce seeds, which can then grow into new agaves under the right circumstances.

Asexual Reproduction by Bulbil

If the flower buds on a quiote are damaged or stressed, bulbils (*bulbillos*) may emerge in their place. Bulbillos look like tinier versions of hijuelos and are also genetic copies of the parent plant.

VEGETATIVE CLONING

These days, a few large agave growers take cuttings from agaves and grow new plants in vitro. These lab-grown baby agaves are guaranteed to be free of pests and are nurtured in greenhouses before being planted in the field.

BLUE AGAVE
WHAT TEQUILA IS MADE OF

If we imagine all Mexican agave spirits as a super-category analogous to wine, tequila is something like a Napa Valley cabernet, made in a particular region from a single varietal of agave. Tequila's primary raw material is the *Agave tequilana* Weber, blue variety, commonly shortened to "blue agave." But this wasn't always the case. For nearly two centuries, what we now call tequila was made from a mix of up to nine agave varietals native to the Tequila Valley. The blue agave emerged among them as the most resistant to a disastrous fungal blight in the late nineteenth century.

Blue agave is endemic to Jalisco, matures in as few as five years (relatively fast compared to other agaves), and contains a large amount of potentially fermentable sugar. Its natural potential as an efficient sugar source was long ago noticed and exploited by humans, who for thousands of years have selected the fastest-growing, sweetest agaves.

By the early twentieth century, blue agave was predominant in tequila production, but six other varietals were still used: *chato, bermejo, sigüin, manolarga, zopilote*, and *pata de mula*. The first law defining tequila, in 1949, specifically mentioned the blue agave but also permitted the use of other agaves "of the same genus" grown in Jalisco (see Tequila History, page 36, and The Denominación de Origen Tequila, page 38).

As tequila continued to industrialize and expand into ever-wider markets, large tequila producers decided to limit agave cultivation to the quickest and highest-yield of the varietals—the blue agave. Limiting their crops to this single type allowed farmers to harvest entire fields at once and tequila makers to make more accurate predictions about how much tequila a ton of agave would yield. The 1964 revision to the tequila law restricted production to blue agave alone.

Opposite page: The characteristic red soil of the Los Altos region where blue agaves are grown.

BLUE AGAVE REPRODUCTION AND SEEKING THE PERFECT PLANT

A healthy blue agave will produce its first "litter" of hijuelos in its second year of life. Most *agaveros* believe that the first- and second-generation hijuelos are superior to those that come later. Hijuelos *de primera* and *de segunda* nearly always find a home. Except in years of shortage, hijuelos of the third generation and beyond generally become compost.

Growers also prefer larger hijuelos and classify their size in reference to common fruits: *piña* (pineapple), *toronja* (grapefruit), *naranja* (orange), and *limón* (lime). When hijuelos are harvested,

their thorny leaves are pruned to turn them into convenient "handles," their roots are lopped off, and their freshly shorn bottom end will be exposed to the sun to dry them out. Best practices also dictate dipping them in a sterilizing fluid to avoid transporting pests from one field to another.

From a farming and tequila-producing perspective, it's easy to see the advantages of cloning. After just two years, farmers can select hijuelos from their best plants, knowing that they have all the positive qualities of the previous generation. With enough land, this allows them to plant each year and to have an annual crop of agave for tequila. Allowing blue agave to flower, become pollinated, and produce seeds would add about two years to the life cycle of each plant, increasing it from a range of five to eight years to a span of seven to ten.

From a tequila-making perspective, allowing the agaves' energy to be used to produce a quiote is a waste of potential booze. So, shortly after the quiote begins to emerge from the heart of the agave, it will be cut off—*capado*, or "castrated." This pruning traps the energy destined for the quiote in the piña. (Harvested quiotes are often cooked, sliced, and eaten as snacks, or milled and made into special tortillas.)

Taking a broader point of view, though, there is a downside to relying on cloning and disallowing sexual reproduction. Cloned agaves will have all the genetic strengths—and weaknesses—of the plant that produced them. On the plus side, this means they grow fast and will produce a lot of tequila. On the downside, cloning stops evolution in its tracks. The agave's natural predators—weevils, fungi, and bacteria—continue to evolve. The agave's weaknesses and susceptibilities are copied and passed down from generation to generation (see Blue Agave Monoculture, page 227). Cutting all the quiotes also removes a food source for the Mexican long-nosed bat. For both reasons, a few producers have begun allowing a small percentage of their agaves to produce quiotes and go to seed to facilitate eventual genetic crosses and to support a healthy population of pollinator bats.

Opposite page: Field workers prepare to plant a new crop of blue agave in the Tequila Valley.

IS TEQUILA
BAD FOR BATS?

Tequila and bats have a surprising relationship that has ecologists and tequila aficionados wondering what they can do to protect the furry nocturnal creatures.

In the wild, flowering agaves rely on insects, birds, and other creatures to facilitate sexual reproduction by carrying pollen from one flower to another. The resulting seeds carry genetic crosses that allow the agave to adapt and evolve. In the case of the *Agave tequilana*, the Mexican long-nosed bat is the primary pollinator. The bats use their long, nimble tongues to extract nectar from agave flowers high in the air, and their fur gets covered in pollen in the process. As they feed on plant after plant, they spread pollen, producing seeds containing new genetic combinations.

The symbiosis between flowering plants and pollinators is a neat trick of nature. One is able to reproduce and ensure the survival of its species, and the other is able to eat and ensure the survival of the individual animal. But the near-universal agricultural practice of severing the quiote in blue agave fields has disrupted the relationship between bats and agaves.

What is certain is that when there are no quiotes, there is no nectar to eat, and bats no longer visit blue agave fields. It's unclear just how much of a problem this is. Some scientists believe this has caused a decline in bat populations, while others say it's possible the bats have simply adapted their migration routes to feed on other flowering plants.

In 2016, Tequila Siembra Azul owner David Suro and bat conservationist Dr. Rodrigo Medellín founded the Bat Friendly Project to certify tequilas that set aside 5% of their agave crops to flower and produce

---

Opposite page: Bats fly by moonlight among agave flower stalks.
Inset: A biologist carefully displays a bat's wingspan.

seeds for planting the next generation of blue agave. The project has brought attention to the issue, but it has struggled to attract participants. One reason is that high agave prices make that 5% loss a very expensive proposition. In the program's first year, three distilleries participated, but no others were certified between 2017 and 2021.

TEQUILA HISTORY
FROM THE BIRTH OF THE MODERN INDUSTRY
TO LEGAL ADULTERATION

1873 The modern tequila industry is born when Cenobio Sauza exports three barrels and six glass *damajuanas* (demijohns) of tequila to El Paso, Texas, by mule train. While some vino mezcal de Tequila had certainly crossed the barely existent northern border previously, this "official" export marks the beginning of a century of Sauza family dominance of the tequila export market. As the end of the nineteenth century nears, the largest tequila producers begin using modern steam-powered equipment: brick ovens, roller mills, and column stills.

1900 TO 1909 As the twentieth century begins, only thirty-nine official tequila distilleries exist, and the count continues to decline during the turbulent first decade. This reduced competition helps the big producers consolidate their control of the market. Exportation to Central America and Europe begins, Mexico inaugurates its first glass bottle factory, and Tequilas Sauza and Cuervo continue to rack up gold medals in international competitions. "Tequila" (sans "mezcal") begins to appear on increasing numbers of tequila labels. The railroad connects Tequila to Mexico City in 1909, allowing for nationwide distribution in durable glass bottles.

1910 TO 1921 The Mexican Revolution kicks off. Agave farming and tequila production stop almost entirely, along with most other agriculture and industry. At the cost of a million deaths, mass starvation, and the decimation of the economy, the revolution achieves nominal land reform. The fractious process of dividing up and redistributing hacienda and Church land will drag on for decades. The tequila industry seems about to disappear as the struggle for survival makes agave growing a null priority for poor farmers.

1929 TO 1935 Jalisco remains in shambles after three years of civil war between the Catholic Church and the federal government. There are only eight working distilleries left in Tequila, but fake tequila is widely available and hurting what is left of the industry's reputation. Legitimate tequila producers begin requesting protection from the federal government. In 1935, the first tequila industry association forms to lobby for their interests.

1940s Mexico exports an unprecedented amount of tequila to the United States in response to wartime and postwar demand. Most of this "tequila" is adulterated with cane liquor to extend the inadequate supply. Tequila makers successfully lobby for the first Mexican law on tequila quality, passed in 1949. It specifies that tequila must be made in Jalisco from 100% mature agave.

1959 TO 1968 Leading *tequileros* found the Regional Chamber of the Tequila Industry (later to become "National"). An agave shortage and surging US demand for tequila coincide to make the 1960s a challenging decade for the industry. The government responds to the shortage by redefining tequila in 1960 and again in 1964, allowing fermentation with non-agave sugars—just what the industry had clamored for protection against in previous decades. The Mexican government underwrites bank loans to farmers who agree to plant agave, and the tragic 1968 Mexico City Olympics introduce tequila to a global audience.

THE DENOMINACIÓN DE ORIGEN TEQUILA
WHERE TEQUILA COMES FROM

All tequila comes from Mexico, and the Mexican government sets the geographic and legal parameters for defining and producing tequila. Over time, these parameters have changed quite a bit, expanding far beyond the Tequila Valley.

Tequila was first defined by a 1949 law that declared that tequila was exclusively from "characteristic" areas of Jalisco state. Later legislation would expand this territory. In 1960, all of Jalisco was included. Unspecified parts of neighboring states with "similar ecological characteristics" were added in 1968.

In 1966, the Lisbon Agreement created an international framework for Geographical Indications (GIs), trade regimes that protect traditional foods and beverages in the global marketplace (see What Is a Denomination of Origin?, page 39). Mexico was one of the original signatories to the agreement, but it wasn't until 1974 that it proclaimed the Denominación de Origen Tequila (DOT) as its first Geographical Indication. Given that the GI concept is predicated on geographic exclusivity, many would have expected tequila's GI to consist exclusively of the Tequila Valley, but at the time of its proclamation, the DOT was the largest GI in the world. (It has since lost that distinction to the mezcal DO.)

The sheer size of tequila's GI has marked it for criticism ever since, especially as it has expanded further. The original 1974 declaration included municipalities in Nayarit, Guanajuato, and Michoacán—all states adjacent to Jalisco. Two years later, Tamaulipas's petition for inclusion was approved, and other minor expansions occurred in 1994 and 2000.

This enlargement underscores tension between the specificity of a unique geocultural region and the capitalist imperative for growth.

Critics of the DOT argue that the latter has long since taken priority, and that no GI of this size can possibly express a true "taste of place," as originally intended. The Tequila Regulatory Council (CRT) and industry leaders counter by arguing that expansion of the DOT and growing tequila sales bring the economic benefits of tequila to a greater number of Mexican families.

WHAT IS A DENOMINATION OF ORIGIN?

Mexican *denominaciones de origen* (DOs) are a type of GI, which is an internationally recognized regime that establishes a monopoly on certain products, usually agricultural, that have been developed within a limited geographical region and cultural context. A GI represents a claim to uniqueness and quality, based on the special characteristics afforded by a specific natural and human environment. GIs, like tequila, often take the name of the place they come from. Other well-known GIs include Cognac, Scotch, Roquefort cheese, and Colombian coffee. GI products are colloquially said to convey "the taste of a place."

GIs are protected by treaties including the General Agreement on Trade and Tariffs (GATT) to which all members of the World Trade Organization (WTO) are signatories.

GIs can be considered a type of intellectual property and may be owned by a collective of producers or by a state. All of Mexico's eighteen GIs belong to the Mexican government. The government determines the specific geographical boundaries and regulations for each of its DOs. In the world of GI research, the DOT is controversial (see A Flawed Geographical Indication, page 226).

The United States, Canada, and Australia do not recognize GIs in the same way that the European Union and most other countries do. These Anglophone countries recognize many, but not all, GIs as a type of trademark. In the United States, the Mexican government is the owner of a "certified mark" for tequila.

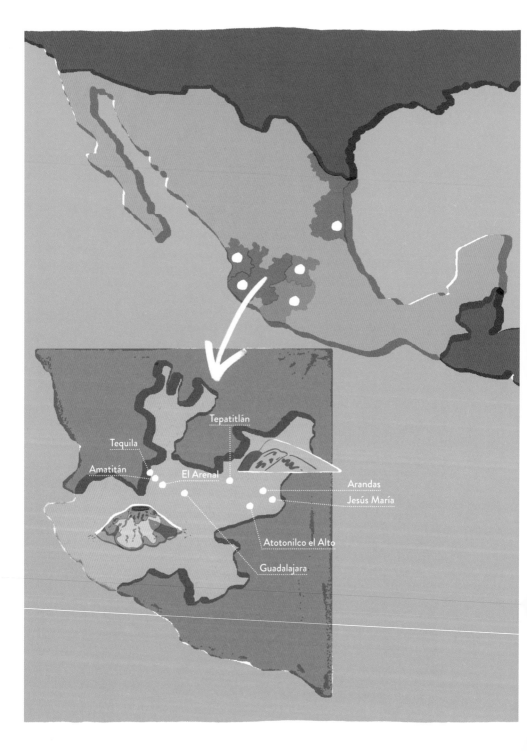

MAPPING THE DOT
JALISCO AND BEYOND

Despite the DOT's massive size, most tequila comes from Jalisco and its 125 municipalities. The state looms large in Mexican culture, as the birthplace not only of tequila but of mariachi music and *charrería* (Mexican rodeo) as well.

Jalisco's primary tequila production regions are the Valle de Tequila and Los Altos regions. They lie on opposite sides of the sprawling state capital of Guadalajara. Los Altos translates literally as "the high places," mirroring "Highlands" in English. While the Tequila Valley is often erroneously called the "Lowlands" in English, in reality the valley is more than 2,000 feet above sea level, and there is no local term that is similar to "Lowlands." The Valley is the birthplace of the tequila tradition. Its primary towns are Tequila, Amatitán, and El Arenal.

The Highlands have been an important source of blue agave for more than 150 years, and began producing tequila in the first half of the twentieth century. Today, the region outpaces the Valley in agave production, and its tequila distilleries continue to proliferate as well. Its primary towns are Arandas, Tepatitlán, Atotonilco el Alto, and Jesús María.

The DOT extends into seven municipalities in Guanajuato, eight in Nayarit, and thirty in Michoacán, all contiguous with Jalisco. This "Jalisco-plus" geographical area was part of Nueva Galicia in the Spanish colonial era. It is arguably a single ecologically and culturally coherent region, artificially broken up by modern state boundaries.

On the other side of the country, the Gulf state of Tamaulipas has eleven municipalities included in the DOT. They were added in a controversial political maneuver as a sop to a powerful Tamaulipas family in 1976 (see The Mystery of Tamaulipas, page 42). To date, their distillery, Chinaco, is one of only two in Tamaulipas.

As of 2023, there are a handful of distilleries in Michoacán, two in Guanajuato, and one in Nayarit. These states are more important as agave producers than tequila makers.

THE MYSTERY
OF TAMAULIPAS

The inclusion of Tamaulipas in the DOT appears initially as an enigma. This Gulf state is hundreds of miles from the Tequila Valley, and it had no claim to the tequila tradition prior to the twentieth century.

Official CRT justifications do little to clarify the issue, as they claim a geographical and cultural resemblance between Tamaulipas and Jalisco that even the casual student of Mexican geography would question. So, what is the real story?

In 1966, Hurricane Inéz decimated the state of Tamaulipas. Farmers experienced massive crop loss, and when wealthy landowner Guillermo González Díaz Lombardo decided to plant blue agave in the aftermath, other farmers followed his lead. They were aware of the wild fluctuations in agave supply and hoped to benefit from the next period of high demand and prices. Tequila industry scion Francisco Javier Sauza had built a distillery in Tamaulipas to produce tequila closer to the US border. He was eager to ensure an agave supply robust enough to meet the increasing global demand for his tequila, and he encouraged the Tamaulipans to plant blue agave. The existing federal tequila rules already limited production to Jalisco, but no regulatory body was charged with enforcing those rules and the DOT did not yet exist.

When the new agave farmers began thinking about harvesting their first crop in 1972, Sauza aggressively sought a far lower price than the prevailing rate. González and the other farmers looked for different buyers in Jalisco, but they were ultimately advised by Guillermo Romo Sr. (then owner of Tequila Herradura, page 142) to instead build their own distillery. González took the advice, and Romo even lent him an engineer, who converted a shuttered cotton gin into the La Gonzaleña distillery in González, Tamaulipas.

Tamaulipas was excluded from the DOT when it was declared in 1974. González and the agave farmers immediately sued. As a descendant of Mexican president Manuel González Flores, González had political connections that reached the highest levels of Mexico's ruling PRI party. He tapped those connections to make a formal bid for Tamaulipas's inclusion in the DOT.

In 1976, newly elected president José López Portillo convened a meeting with tequila industry leaders to find a resolution to the Tamaulipas issue. There were now 50 million blue agaves planted in the state, and La Gonzaleña was ready to start making "tequila de Tamaulipas." The expansion effort was vigorously opposed by most in the industry, now including Francisco Javier Sauza, who was presumably still angry about the failed agave purchase. In a still mysterious about-face, Sauza abandoned plans for the border distillery and presented himself as a great defender of Jalisco, staunchly opposed to admitting the faraway region he had recently wanted to make tequila in himself. Guillermo Romo supported the Tamaulipas proposal for equally obscure reasons. The ensuing brouhaha became heated and resulted in Sauza's dramatic ejection from the meeting by President López Portillo.

Eleven municipalities in Tamaulipas were admitted to the DOT in 1976. The reasons enumerated in the government declaration are telling. In contrast to the CRT's later insistence on some cultural or ecological similarity between Jalisco and Tamaulipas, the government found that the tequila "industrials" of Jalisco were responsible for fomenting blue agave planting in Tamaulipas; the agave planted was "acceptable" for tequila production; a considerable amount of money had been invested; there was potential for development and job creation; and a greater supply of agave was needed to meet rising international demand and to avoid an increase in *mixto* production (see The Return of Quality Mixtos, page 64).

The expansion of the DOT to Tamaulipas was a pragmatic realization of an economic investment by a prestigious family, growing demand, and a certain sense of justice for those who had been induced to plant blue agave for the tequila industry. For critics, the DOT's "original sin" illustrates that its primary goals are economic development, increased exports, and job creation—not the expression of terroir or preservation of traditional culture or the natural environment so often touted as the sine qua non of GIs.

TEQUILA HISTORY
FROM ESTABLISHMENT OF THE DOT
TO A TRUE GLOBAL SPIRIT

1974 Industry leaders celebrate as Mexico declares the Denomination of Origin for Tequila (DOT). Tequila reposado is classified and defined. Mexico successfully negotiates the suppression of pseudo-tequilas in various countries.

1980 TO 1990s Mexico's economy suffers and widespread bacterial and fungal infections decimate agave fields. Large tequila producers begin seeking long-term contracts with agave growers to ensure supply. In 1991, inability to meet demand becomes so dire that tequila with as little as 30% agave is approved for production behind closed doors.

1994 TO 2010s The contemporary tequila category

comes to life as the Mexican government authorizes the Tequila Regulatory Council (CRT) to enforce the Official Mexican Norm on Tequila (NOM) within the DOT. In 1994, the United States formally recognizes Mexico's exclusive right to produce tequila, and the European Union follows suit three years later. The entire focus of the industry shifts to exports and international promotion.

Late 1990s TO early 2000s The

US boom in 100% agave "sipping" tequila is on, fueled by the craft cocktail movement's insistence on quality ingredients. A 1997 snowstorm wipes out or weakens most of the young agave in the Los Altos region. An opportunistic invasion by pests follows, causing a drastic decline in agave supply and a jump in price. Overplanting results, and cheap agave begins to flood the market in 2010. With tequila's unprecedented global presence, the agave is bought up by a bevy of new brands, and a distillery construction boom begins.

2020s AND beyond The tequila industry is

much larger than it's ever been: More than 140 distilleries produce more than 2,000 brands for a total of 527 million liters in 2021. Most of that tequila is made by the five largest brands and will end up in cocktails. At the other end of the spectrum, a few dozen tiny distilleries produce a small volume of coveted "craft" tequila, much of which will be sipped neat. These tequileros can charge a premium for quality and are envied and emulated by the rest of the industry. Some industry observers predict that tequila sales will overtake both American whiskey and vodka sales in the United States in 2023.

THE NORMA OFICIAL MEXICANA AND THE CONSEJO REGULADOR DEL TEQUILA
HOW TEQUILA IS DEFINED

While issues of regulation may initially seem boring, they are an interesting part of what makes tequila unique. It's important to understand the basics.

The Mexican government owns and defines the Denomination of Origin for Tequila (DOT), and the government also establishes a set of rules that govern the whole tequila industry. These rules are called the Norma Oficial Mexicana—006-SCFI-2012, Bebidas alcohólicas—Tequila—Especificaciones, known simply as "the Norm" by tequila aficionados, and they are interpreted and enforced by an independent regulatory body called the Consejo Regulador del Tequila (CRT, or Tequila Regulatory Council). The CRT is authorized by the state and funded by the industry.

The CRT's application of the Norm is arguably the strictest regulatory system in all of distilled spirits. Its enforcement begins soon after the agave is planted. Verification extends through the tequila-making process and continues all the way into bottling and labeling. The CRT and NOM logos on every tequila label indicate that the tequila was produced in accordance with the Norm under the supervision of the CRT.

WHAT'S WITH ALL THE ACRONYMS?
THE ABC'S OF TEQUILA

The "what," "where," and "how" of tequila making involve a lot of potentially confusing acronyms. Use this table as a cheat sheet to keep track of what is what.

GI: Geographical Indication	The generic term for the protected status enjoyed by products that by law can be produced only in a specific area. Champagne, Scotch whisky, and Darjeeling tea are GIs, protected by the General Agreement on Tariffs and Trade. Individual countries may refer to their GIs by different names.
DO: Denominación de Origen	Mexico calls its Geographical Indications DOs. As of 2023, Mexico had declared eighteen DOs, although not all of them have been internationally recognized. These DOs are owned by the state and are recognized through the Mexican Institute for Industrial Property (IMPI).
DOT: Denominación de Origen Tequila	In 1974, the DO for tequila (DOT) became the world's first non-European GI. It established the geographical boundaries of tequila production, which have been expanded over time.
NOM: Norma Oficial Mexicana	NOMs are administrative "norms," or rules, that govern most sectors of Mexico's economy. In the context of tequila, the Norm technically refers to NOM—006-SCFI-2012, Bebidas alcohólicas—Tequila—Especificaciones. This Norm defines tequila and establishes rules for making it.
CRT: Consejo Regulador del Tequila	The Tequila Regulatory Council (CRT) is a nonprofit authorized by the Mexican state to inspect and certify tequila distilleries in accordance with the tequila NOM. Tequila is not tequila unless and until the CRT says it is.

THE CRT

The CRT is often referred to as "the tequila police" because it oversees compliance with the Norm. That is fair enough, but the CRT could also be thought of as "the tequila Supreme Court" because it interprets the meaning of the Norm when disagreements arise. The CRT has a lot of power in the tequila industry.

The Mexican government authorizes the CRT to oversee all aspects of tequila production, conduct laboratory analysis, and certify legitimate tequila in what is called a "system of permanent verification." The CRT mission also includes safeguarding the DOT and promoting tequila worldwide.

AGRICULTURAL ENFORCEMENT

Farmers usually plant agaves in early summer at the beginning of the rainy season. The farmer has until the end of the year to report the planting to the CRT. The CRT uses satellite imaging to add the newly planted agave to its inventory and numbers each plant. Every year, farmers are required to file a report with the CRT specifying what percentage of their agaves are healthy, are sick, have been destroyed, or have been harvested.

While imperfect in execution, the intent is to know the amount of available raw material in any given year and thus have a rough idea of how much tequila to expect five to eight years later when those agaves mature. The yearly monitoring is also intended to discourage tricks, such as planting one year, then pulling up the agave, farming other crops for a few years, then suddenly presenting agave from some mysterious source. Because of the agave's long growing cycle, farmers don't see a return on their investment for years, so these kinds of practices are tempting when times are tough. When the agave is harvested and transported to a distillery, it is issued a CRT "passport" for the same reasons.

DISTILLERY INSPECTIONS

CRT verifiers are empowered to inspect and document all aspects of any tequilero's process, day or night. The large producers have permanent offices for CRT verifiers, who are at the distillery every day. Verifiers are rotated out from time to time to prevent relationships between producers and CRT officials from becoming too cozy. Even the smallest distilleries may receive a visit from the CRT every day that they are working, especially if they're in the distillery-dense Tequila Valley.

Tequila is rested or aged in oak to make *reposado, añejo,* or *extra-añejo* (see page 52). It may also be stored in stainless steel for weeks or months before bottling. CRT verifiers seal oak barrels and steel tanks when they are filled with tequila. They do this to guarantee the aging time and class of the tequila. The quantity, date, and category of tequila are logged. A verifier's permission is required to breach the seal for any reason. So, if the producer wants to bottle, blend, taste, or otherwise examine the tequila, they have to get the go-ahead from the CRT. If the seal is broken without permission, the contents may be delicious and will almost certainly be consumed, but they will never be legally sold as tequila.

LABORATORY ANALYSIS

Every batch of tequila bottled undergoes analysis at a CRT-approved laboratory. This applies equally to the 200 million liters a year produced by José Cuervo and to the 10,000 liters a year produced by a small family operation. Through lab analysis, the CRT guarantees that all tequila contains acceptable amounts of potentially dangerous substances: ethyl alcohol (that's the fun stuff), methanol ("bad" alcohol), superior alcohols, esters, aldehydes, furfurals, and "dry extract" (see Aging Tequila, page 112). The CRT guarantees that all tequila is safe to drink in moderate amounts.

A sample or "witness" of each batch of tequila certified is kept by the CRT for at least one year. Hypothetically, any bottle of tequila can be traced back to its lab results and even all the way back to the date and field where the agave it was made from was planted.

THE NORM

The Tequila Norm is one of hundreds of "Official Norms" governing most Mexican industries. This Norm "establishes the characteristics and specifications" that must be adhered to by the entire agave-tequila production chain, from field to retail. But the most important part of the Norm is defining the categories and classes of tequila.

TWO CATEGORIES OF TEQUILA

There are two categories of tequila. One is simply called "tequila" and the other is called "100% agave tequila." If that seems a little bit confusing to you, you're not alone.

	100% AGAVE TEQUILA	TEQUILA (AKA "MIXTO")
SUGAR SOURCE	100% blue agave	At least 51% blue agave
PRODUCTION AND BOTTLING	Must be made and bottled in the DOT	Must be made in the DOT
CERTIFIED BY CRT	Yes	Yes
HOW TO IDENTIFY THE PRODUCT ON THE SHELF OR SEALS TO LOOK FOR	Labeled as "100% agave tequila" or "tequila 100% agave"	Labeled as "tequila"; will not say "100%" or "mixto"

The term "100% agave tequila" means that 100% of the tequila's alcohol is derived from fermented blue agave sugar. Period. It does not mean that there are no other ingredients in the tequila. This category of tequila can be fermented with chemical enhancements, and it can contain additives (see All About Additives, page 56). "100% agave" is solely a statement about the sugar source.

A bottle simply labeled "tequila" contains alcohol derived from at least 51% blue agave and up to 49% other sugar. This category is known as mixto tequila. But the term "mixto" is not in the Norm, and it won't be found on any label. The CRT considers it to be derogatory, although it is a literal description of the sugar source.

Historically, the other sugars in mixto were some form of cane sugar from Jalisco. These days, the largest tequila producers use high fructose corn syrup imported from the United States.

Mixtos are often misunderstood as something like blends of tequila and rum, given the "other sugars." However, "cold blends" of tequila and another finished spirit are explicitly prohibited by the Norm. The non-agave sugars in a mixto are added to the cooked agave juice in formulation, just prior to fermentation (see Formulation, page 93).

The Norm makes another crucial distinction between tequila (mixto) and 100% agave tequila. Mixtos may be exported from Mexico in bulk at 55% ABV and diluted and bottled anywhere in the world. 100% agave tequila must be bottled at between 35% and 55% ABV within the DOT territory. This gives mixtos a significant competitive advantage overseas because freight costs will be lower. Diluted, bottled 100% agave tequila includes glass and water—both very heavy—while mixto is shipped in massive tankers at the maximum ABV allowed by law. This advantage is furthered by the CRT's insistence that both categories of tequila are equal in quality.

Two bottles of reposado: one "tequila" and one "100% agave tequila."

THE FIVE CLASSES OF TEQUILA

E ach of tequila's two categories is further divided into five classes, giving a total of ten possible types of tequila. Classes essentially indicate how long, if at all, the tequila has been rested or aged in oak.

	BLANCO/PLATA	REPOSADO	AÑEJO	EXTRA-AÑEJO	JOVEN/ORO
CATEGORY (tequila or 100% agave tequila)	Can be either	Can be either	Can be either	Can be either, usually 100% agave tequila	Can be either, usually tequila
TIME IN OAK	Less than two months (usually unaged)	Two months minimum	One year minimum	Three years minimum	A blend of blanco and one or more other categories or a blanco with additives
AGING VESSEL	Any oak (rare)	Any oak	Oak barrel of 600 liters or less	Oak barrel of 600 liters or less	N/A

BLANCO OR PLATA. Blancos typically have no contact whatsoever with wood but are allowed to be in contact with oak for up to two months. Few producers rest their blanco in oak, and the more traditional producers never do.

Blanco tequilas are sometimes supplemented with marketing terms like "platino," "platinum," "crystal," etc. These are allowed, but they have no meaning per the Norm. Their labels will also say "blanco," "plata," or "silver" as the official class name.

There is a persistent myth that blancos must be bottled within a certain maximum time after distillation, and this is completely false. Tequila may be stored indefinitely in inert materials like stainless steel between distillation and bottling.

Some people insist that blancos are harsh, hot, aggressive, and good only for mixing or taking shots. This is an unfortunate myth, perpetuated by producers of inferior tequilas. Blancos are actually the purest expression of both the agave and the distiller's craft. It is the baseline by which we judge a product line. After all, blancos are the basic building block of all the other classes produced in a distillery. There is no hiding flaws in a blanco, and they are the first tequilas reached for by purists and aficionados.

REPOSADO. This "rested" class of tequila has been in contact with oak for more than two months. Reposados can be rested in oak containers of any size: There is no maximum volume. Some reposados are rested in wooden tanks called *pipones* rather than barrels. Pipones as large as 10,000 liters are currently in use. Such a large volume imparts less intense woody notes than aging in smaller barrels does.

Many consider reposados to be the most difficult class of tequila to make well. At their best, reposados exhibit a keen balance between the fresh, raw aspects of a blanco and the dark, sweet notes of an oak barrel. The risk is that they may end up in a bland middle ground, neither here nor there, a toned-down version of a blanco that doesn't quite have the complexity and approachability of a more aged tequila. But well-made reposados can be truly beautiful and can provide an accessible and budget-friendly entry point for new tequila drinkers.

AÑEJO. Añejo is an old-timey Spanish word for "year old," and these tequilas spend at least one year in oak. Añejos are aged in barrels, and the maximum size is 600 liters. In practice, most are aged in smaller 200-liter used American whiskey barrels.

After a year in an oak barrel, tequila usually begins to drink more like a whiskey or other brown spirit. Añejos therefore attract drinkers of other aged spirits, who may or may not come to appreciate the purity of unaged tequilas. Because of the "angel's share" lost during aging (see Is Aged Tequila Better?, page 116), there is a significant jump in price from reposado to añejo tequila.

EXTRA-AÑEJO. The newest class of tequila (added to the Norm in 2006) spends a minimum of three years in an oak barrel. As with añejos, the barrel can be no larger than 600 liters.

Everything said about the appeal of añejos goes double for extra-añejos. Their exclusive price points also make them status symbols and impressive gifts. Years ago, most tequila makers argued there was no point in aging tequila more than four or five years, given the angel's share and the decrease in agave aromas and flavors over time. But as tequila attracts more (and wealthier) drinkers of brown spirits like whiskies, there seems to be no upper limit on how long producers will age tequila: In 2014 Fuenteseca (page 160) released a twenty-one-year-old extra-añejo!

JOVEN OR ORO. These "gold" tequilas are a blend of blanco and one or more of the other classes. While many have negative associations with these tequilas, they are being reintroduced in the 100% agave category. Blending from as many as four classes of their own tequila provides producers with nearly limitless potential in the creation of a unique aged tequila flavor profile.

BLENDING AGED TEQUILAS

There is no upper limit to the time that reposados, añejos, and extra-añejos spend in oak. The Norm dictates the minimum for these classes. Blanco is the only category that is also defined by a maximum.

A tequila that has been in a small oak barrel for one year may be called an añejo, but it doesn't have to be. Of course, there is a strong incentive for the producer to label and sell it as an añejo, because it can command a higher price than a reposado. However, occasionally a tequilero wants an oakier-than-average reposado and may allow some or all of it to go past the one-year mark. They may likewise allow an añejo to stay in the barrel a little more than three years, even though doing so will make it a more expensive añejo.

The fact that there is no maximum on aged tequilas is key to understanding how blending different classes works. First, the easy one: A blanco blended with any rested or aged tequila becomes a joven. But when different classes of rested or aged tequila are blended, the resulting tequila is defined by the least aged tequila in the blend. If there is any reposado (but no blanco) in a blend, it is a reposado. Likewise, if there is any añejo in a blend (but no blanco or reposado), it is an añejo.

So, a reposado may have any amount of a more aged tequila (añejo, extra-añejo, or both) blended into it. It is the presence of any reposado that makes the whole batch a reposado. This is a technique for adding an extra punch of oak to a reposado (see Aging Tequila, page 112).

We can imagine an absurd hypothetical scenario in which someone carelessly spills a cup of reposado into a 1,000-liter tank of extra-añejo. That cup of reposado has now turned the entire vat into a (very expensive) reposado! In a more likely scenario, this rule prevents producers from doing the opposite: adding a tiny amount of extra-añejo, for example, to a reposado, and calling that blend an extra-añejo.

Opposite page: Typical hues of the five classes of tequila: blanco/plata, oro/joven, reposado, añejo, and extra-añejo.

ALL ABOUT ADDITIVES

Natural, old-school tequilas are made with three ingredients: agave, water, and yeast. Many people assume that the "100% agave tequila" designation denotes such a tequila. But that category refers only to the fermented sugar source. These days, all tequilas are allowed to contain a certain quantity of additives to enhance flavor, aroma, color, and mouthfeel.

Four specific "mellowing" additives—*abocantes* in Spanish—are explicitly allowed in all classes of tequila except blanco: caramel, for color and sweetness; glycerin, for sweetness and mouthfeel; oak extract, to mimic some of the effects of barrel aging; and syrup—for sweetness and flavor. The Norm further allows all tequilas, including blancos, to contain any "sweeteners, colorants, aromas, and/or flavorings" approved for use in Mexico by the Secretariat of Health. There are limits to the volume of additives that can be used, but the intense strength of twenty-first-century additives renders these limits almost meaningless.

Tequila brands that use abocantes and sweeteners do not have to disclose their presence on the label or anywhere else. While some purists would prefer a total prohibition on additives in tequila, it is the lack of disclosure that gets the goat of many aficionados.

Responding to widespread consumer demand for information on additives, Tequila Matchmaker (see page 190) in 2020 created a Confirmed Additive-Free program, which is completely independent and voluntary. Distilleries or brands that opt in to the program commit to complete transparency: Matchmaker physically inspects distilleries, reviews production records, and conducts organoleptic analysis in order to confirm that a brand or distillery does not use additives in its tequila. There is no obligation to participate in the program, and presumably some non-additive distilleries do not do so. Nevertheless, Matchmaker's regularly updated list is the most reliable source for people who are looking for additive-free tequilas.

FLAVORED TEQUILAS

Flavored tequilas were introduced to the tequila Norm in 2012. One hundred percent agave tequila may contain additives, and these do not have to be disclosed on the label. However, if those additives pass a certain CRT threshold, the tequila must be labeled as "flavored," and the type of flavoring must be listed on the label. Often, this is part of the brand's planned identity, as for strawberry- and jalapeño-flavored tequilas. But sometimes a tequila producer goes too far for the CRT and is forced to disclose the sweeteners or flavorings they had been using all along—as happened with Herradura Cristalino.

THE TEQUILA NAME GAME

The Tequila Norm is a government document, and as you might expect, its language is far from clear and consistent. One of the areas where this is most true is in the names of tequila's classes.

The original and largest class of tequila has two names: blanco and plata. However, this is one single, unitary class and those terms (and the English "silver") may be used interchangeably. Some tequila brands have both a blanco and a silver on the market. For example, Herradura blanco (produced specifically for the Mexican market) is totally unaged and bottled at 46% ABV. Herradura silver (available throughout the world) is rested in oak for about forty-five days and bottled at 40% ABV. It is important to understand that Herradura could label the two products in the exact opposite manner, as the two terms are completely interchangeable.

There is a similar issue with the joven, or oro, class (also "gold" in English): two names, a single class. Overconsumption of some infamous mass-produced mixto golds in the 1970s and 1980s left a whole generation of Americans with negative associations with this class of tequila. However, there has been a small early-twenty-first-century comeback of 100% agave versions of this class. To avoid stirring up memories of the bad old days, these are usually labeled joven.

Finally, the official English translations for the other three classes are potentially confusing and therefore usually ignored. The Norm states that "aged" is the official translation for reposado, "extra-aged" for añejo, and "ultra-aged" for extra-añejo. Given the potential confusion caused by using "extra" in two distinct classes, the original Spanish terms are almost always used on labels in English-speaking countries. Informally, the broader tequila industry has long since settled on "rested," "aged," and "extra-aged" as synonyms for reposado, añejo, and extra-añejo.

LABELING AND TRACEABILITY

By law, tequila labels are required to display certain information, including category and class, logos of the CRT and NOM, the four-digit number of the producer, some version of "Made in Mexico," and the authorized importer. The rules about the size, font, and placement of these details are quite specific. Each bottle is also required to carry the production lot (or batch) number of the tequila inside. The Norm doesn't specify how or where the lot number is to be displayed. Some small brands, like Fortaleza (page 168), make the lot number an integral part of the label and their brand identity. Aficionados avidly taste and rate each individual lot, developing favorites and theories about minor variations in flavor profile. More commonly, the lot number is machine-stamped on the inside of the label and can be seen only by looking through the bottle. Whether it is obvious or hard to find, that number makes it theoretically possible for the CRT to trace any bottle of tequila all the way back to the field that supplied the agave.

The CRT doesn't claim to guarantee that any particular tequila is good. That's a subjective judgment and is left up to each consumer. What the CRT ultimately guarantees is that what is on the label is true: that what's in that bottle was produced within the DOT, in accordance with the Norm, under the aegis of the CRT. The CRT further guarantees that the category and class on the label are accurate. Defining tequila's two categories and five classes is one of the most important functions of the Norm.

WHAT'S IN A NOM NUMBER?

Every tequila label bears the acronyms CRT and NOM, ensuring consumers that what's in the bottle was produced in accordance with the Tequila Norm, under the auspices of the CRT. A four-digit number also appears between "CRT" and "NOM." Because of this placement, aficionados call it the "NOM number" (or just "the NOM"), although these numbers aren't technically regulated by the Norm or the CRT.

The NOM number identifies the producer responsible for the tequila in the bottle and provides clues as to what the tequila might taste like. NOM numbers are commonly believed to be synonymous with individual distilleries. Indeed, even among producers that make a dozen or more brands (see page 130), most use the same NOM for all the brands they make. But there are exceptions.

The Mexican government issues NOM numbers to business entities, which aren't necessarily the distilleries themselves. Various business entities associated with a single distillery may acquire their own numbers. For example, most of the tequilas made at Campo Azul bear the number 1416, although Teramana (1613) and Clase Azul (1595) are both made there. Conversely, Casa Cuervo's 1122 NOM doesn't tell us whether the contents were made at their massive Los Camichines distillery or the smaller La Rojeña facility.

There is another, more important detail regarding NOM numbers. Certified tequila producers can sell each other bulk tequila with CRT permission. This tequila can be blended into a larger batch or bottled and sold as is. While the process is monitored by the CRT, the information is not publicly accessible. These purchases are especially common when aged tequilas are scarce and in demand—around holidays, for example. While some producers proudly bottle just their own tequila, the number on the label ultimately only tells us who is responsible for that tequila. There could be tequila from multiple producers blended in any one bottle, which complicates the CRT's commitment to traceability.

CRISTALINO TEQUILAS
WHAT ARE THEY?

Cristalino tequilas are surging in popularity, so it may seem odd that the word doesn't appear as a category, class, or in fact anywhere in the Norm. The status of these novel tequilas is up in the air and likely to provoke significant debate the next time the Norm is revised. "Cristalino" is a commonly used term for aged tequilas that have been made totally colorless—usually by filtration but occasionally by a post-aging distillation.

In 2008, José Cuervo launched the Maestro Dobel brand, a tequila that quietly announced an innovation that would shake up the industry. The Dobel product (named after the nickname of Cuervo heir Juan Domingo Beckman) was a joven tequila, but it was filtered with charcoal, which rendered it completely transparent, like an unaged blanco. This technique had been used in the rum industry for some time. Dobel was a successful product, but at the time few consumers paid attention to its unique production.

Dobel was followed by a clear-filtered añejo called Don Julio 70 (DJ70), released for the brand's seventieth anniversary. DJ70 captured consumers' imaginations in a way Dobel hadn't. Serious tequila aficionados knew that añejos were supposed to be brown, yet here was one from a renowned brand that was clear.

That confusion is part of what leads purists to be skeptical of cristalinos. Such critics argue that the charcoal filtration that removes color also strips the tequila of aromas and flavors imparted by oak aging, which are subsequently replaced with additives.

On its face, the whole process does lead to some head-scratching. With cristalinos, the color, aroma, and flavor acquired from months or years in a barrel is deliberately stripped away in a process that costs money and results in some product loss (to filtration). Then, in most cases additives are used, and the cost of production is increased even more.

Cynics further contend that the origin of cristalinos was more about unloading a glut of slow-selling aged tequilas than anything else. It is true that the original cristalinos were launched after years of low agave prices, which had led to millions more liters of aged tequila than the market could bear. So, it is plausible that cristalinos were initially just a clever way to repackage and unload aged tequila that was taking up space. If so, the strategy has worked so well that añejos and extra-añejos are in short supply as of 2023, due in part to rising demand for cristalinos.

From the initial trickle of cristalinos, around half the industry now produces or has plans to produce one. Proponents argue that cristalinos have all the "smoothness" acquired in aging, with the crisp cleanness of a silver tequila. More importantly, they point to rising consumer demand for clear-filtered tequilas as proof enough of the idea's validity, purists be damned.

Like it or not, cristalinos are here to stay. It's widely expected that they will be codified in the Norm the next time the rules are revised. Until that happens, cristalino remains a marketing term with no specific definition, and these tequilas must therefore also be labeled as one of the five currently recognized classes of tequila.

Bottles of cristalino tequilas. Brands emphasize the tequila's transparency with stark black-and-white labels.

TEQUILA AS MEZCAL

The success of more traditional tequilas is driving the back-to-basics trend of producers returning to their mezcal de Tequila roots.

Originally, tequila was one of many regional mezcals. For historical reasons, tequila became famous, shed the mezcal label, and became a category unto itself. For more than a century, tequileros went to great pains to distinguish tequila from what they considered the cruder, inferior mezcals made under primitive conditions. But this is starting to change.

Mezcal from Oaxaca captured the imaginations of urban Mexicans in the early part of this century. Its aromatic complexity and rustic production offered a contrast to banal, mass-produced spirits—including many tequilas. This "mezcal boom" caused many a tequila aficionado to denounce Jalisco's blue agave liquor and declare themselves for mezcal only. In the first two decades of the twenty-first century, the minuscule mezcal market increased tenfold, growing to 2% of tequila's total volume. The tequila industry took notice, and many tequileros assumed that the growth of mezcal was coming at the expense of tequila sales. Something had to be done to protect their territory.

The responses of tequila producers have ranged from the superficial (like adding smoke flavor to tequila) to the profound: the reintroduction of earthen pit ovens to tequila making after more than a century (see page 84).

Hard-core tequila fans' obsession with comparing flavors resulting from distinct terroir and production techniques has been reinforced by mezcal culture's longstanding recognition of the individuals and communities that produce the spirit and differentiation based on region, agave varietal, and production methods. Tequila Ocho, for example, made the agave's growing region part of its tequila's identity (page 164); this has been commonplace in mezcal for centuries. As mezcal's growing popularity encourages the tequila industry to acknowledge its own history as a regional mezcal, more producers are identifying the source of their agave and making production techniques and their "master distiller" part of their brand identities.

THE RETURN
OF QUALITY MIXTOS

The (non–100% agave) "tequila" category is commonly known as "mixto," despite the CRT's opposition to the term. Originally, mixtos were made from a 70/30 blend of agave and some type of local cane sugar—often *piloncillo*, an unprocessed, flavorful brown sugar. That standard was lowered to 51/49 in 1970. With increasing industrialization and US-Mexico trade, cheap American corn syrup has become the sugar source of choice for large tequila producers.

For decades, most serious tequila aficionados have opposed mixtos on principle. Insisting on 100% agave tequila and encouraging others to do the same became the main badge of tequila knowledge. Some might concede to economic considerations and tolerate a mixto in margaritas, but they would insist on *puros* for sipping.

All this is still mostly true, but the disdain for at least certain mixtos has begun to diminish a bit. The change is mostly negatively motivated: Increased diffuser production (see Diffusers, page 87) and additive use in the 100% agave category mean that avoiding mixtos is no longer a guarantee of getting a traditional tequila. Once upon a time, you could blow minds simply by having people compare any 100% agave tequila to the cheap gold mixto people were used to. Nowadays, not so much. For every reliable, budget-friendly 100% agave sipper like Pueblo Viejo or Cimarrón, there are now a dozen insipid diffuser tequilas made with 100% immature agave and sweeteners. The 100% category itself is sadly not the mark of quality it once was.

Consequently, many aficionados and bartenders are going back to better-made mixtos, especially for cocktails. There is no better example than El Tequileño's (NOM 1108) flagship blanco mixto. Made with mature Highland agaves in Tequila, it is the semi-official house pour at Cantina La Capilla (see page 214). The Salles family that produces Tequileño has staunchly maintained the historic 70% agave, 30% piloncillo formula out of respect for tradition. That means it lacks the thin mouthfeel and quick finish of many other, more industrially produced mixtos.

Others have taken note, and a growing number of distilleries are moving away from corn syrup and going back to more natural sugars for their mixtos. It remains to be seen if this will become a real movement, but given the degradation of the 100% agave category, there will be room for quality mixtos well into the foreseeable future. One simultaneously obvious but mind-blowing point: The 49% "other sugars" allowance doesn't have to be from derivatives of corn or sugar cane. Mexico is blessed with an outrageous diversity of fruits, many of which, like mangoes, have extremely high sugar levels and have been fermented and distilled for centuries. While processing and fermenting fruit with agave is significantly more expensive than using cane sugar, quiet experiments are already under way.

El Tequileño blanco, a classic, quality ("mixto") tequila that remains a local favorite in Tequila, Jalisco.

CHAPTER 2

MAKING TEQUILA

FROM FIELD TO BOTTLE

HOW IS TEQUILA MADE?

magine you have been served two glasses of tequila, side by side, and are asked which you prefer. The one on the left is crystal clear, the one on the right is a translucent gold. You smell and then taste each tequila, one at a time. The first tequila smells earthy, herbal, and green. When sipped, there's a surprising balance of vegetal sweetness and black licorice. The flavors quickly fade into a pleasant, tingling astringency. It's good! The second tequila has strong aromas of vanilla, mint, and baking spices you can't quite name. You take another sip and now also perceive black cherry and hazelnut. The tequila feels silky smooth in your mouth, and the flavors linger a long while. It's also good.

You aren't quite sure which one you prefer. They are both delicious, and each is completely distinct. If you hadn't been told they were both tequilas, you might say they had nothing in common. It turns out you tasted an artisanally produced blanco from Amatitán in the Tequila Valley, and an añejo from one of the largest distilleries in Los Altos. Both were made from the blue agave plant, in Jalisco, according to the rules of the Tequila Norm and under the aegis of the Tequila Regulatory Council. How can two tequilas be so radically different?

The Norm prescribes few details about how tequila is actually made. Essentially, all tequila is made in the same way. First, blue agave is harvested. The agave is then cooked, and its starchy carbohydrates are converted into sugar. That sugar is diluted and fermented. The fermented liquid is distilled into tequila, which may then be aged in oak or rested, diluted, filtered, and bottled.

But the devil is in the details. Each of these steps presents options to the tequilero. The myriad possibilities at each step combine for nearly limitless permutations of hypothetical tequilas that could be produced by the same person with the same equipment. Choices made at each step will affect the ultimate flavor profile of the tequila. Multiply this by approximately 140 distilleries, and you can begin to understand the potential breadth and depth of tequila.

A tequilero confronts these choices with three goals in mind: to make a profit, to make a tasty beverage, and to legally certify that beverage as a tequila. Objectively, a tequila is going to have to pass laboratory muster at the CRT. It will need to be within legally established parameters for a number of chemical compounds formed during production. Subjectively, the tequilero wants the tequila to taste good. They may even have a specific vision about what "good tequila" means and may seek to express that through specific choices in production. Those choices may be guided by family traditions, scientific analysis, gut intuition, or some combination of the three. The possibilities are limited by the final objective factor: cost. Some processes or techniques are more expensive than others, and even the most artfully minded distiller has to pay attention to what the market will bear.

In theory, it is possible to make an infinite number of tequilas. That diversity begins with the blue agave itself—a gift from nature. Nature conspires with fermentation to turn simple flavors into complex ones. The seeming magic of fermentation gives way to the art of distillation, where the producer takes full control of the process and strives to realize a vision, constrained by the external realities of regulation and consumers' willingness to spend.

PRODUCTION OF TEQUILA

1 Agave cultivation
2 Agave harvest
3 Hydrolysis
4 Extraction
5 Fermentation
6 Distillation
7 Aging
8 Bottling

AGAVE CULTIVATION

Blue agave is the main ingredient in tequila. Nature provides everything the agave needs to grow, thrive, and hoard massive amounts of energy. Years later, that energy will burst forth as tequila drinkers take over dance floors, sob at funerals, and high-five at baptisms and graduations. To get from a baby agave plant to an adult beverage of complexity and sophistication, nature must intervene for five to eight years . . . with the help of a lot of labor.

All tequila—expensive and cheap, good and bad—is an agricultural product. It starts with plants, and each of those plants is harvested by hand. Every drop of tequila represents the entire life cycle of a noble agave: birth, years of struggle to grow, reproduction, and death. Every drop of tequila represents years of hard work and sweat under the unrelenting sun. Every drop of tequila deserves respect, whether you happen to prefer the taste of that particular drop or not.

The yearslong journey from field to glass starts with the humble hijuelo (a "pup," or offset). These are the clones produced annually by growing agaves (see Agave Reproduction, page 28).

AGAVE PLANTING

When hijuelos are transplanted between fields, they are thirsty. It may have been weeks or months since they were uprooted, pruned, and left out to dry and "scar" in the blazing spring sun. This is by design, because "thirsty" plants will quickly seek out any available water. The hijuelos are planted about a meter apart from one another, with three meters between each row. As soon as the summer rains come, the agave's ancient genetic code activates its root tissues, and the tiny plantlets put everything they have into spreading as many lateral roots as possible just beneath the surface of the soil. This allows the root lattice to absorb the daily torrential downpours that quickly pass through the topsoil and into the deeper recesses of the earth. The agave's struggle to live won't get any easier than this, though, because once the rains end in September, the plants will receive hardly any water until the following summer.

AGAVE GROWTH

Agaves aren't the only thirsty plants in the neighborhood, and summer's sun and rain showers bring a proliferation of grasses and shrubs, all of which are considered weeds by the agave farmer. These plants compete with the agave for sunshine and soil nutrients and may provide a habitat for harmful insects. In their first years of life, agaves are vulnerable to being choked out by other plants, so weed control is crucial. This is done with herbicides, manual weeding with the *coa de limpieza* (a razor-sharp hoe), or both.

The soil provides agave with mineral nutrients needed for growth, and crop rotation, fertilization, or both are necessary to replenish it. Fertilizers can be chemical products or organic matter. A regimen of fertilization reduces the time required for the agave to reach maturity, and increases its ultimate sugar yield, which determines how much tequila it can produce.

A crop of blue agave will be tended by a crew of field workers a few days a year for five to ten years, until the plants are ready to be harvested. From year two onward, workers use a blunt, long-handled tool called a *barretón* to separate hijuelos from parent plants. These hijuelos are transplanted, and another cycle of planting begins.

In nature, the last phase of the blue agave's life is inflorescence. Farmed blue agave won't be allowed to flower, however. When the flower stalk (quiote) emerges, it will be severed. Many plants are also harvested as *novillos*—plants considered mature despite not having produced a quiote. For tequila-production purposes, agave maturity is a matter of carbohydrate content. Agaves will reach maturity five to ten years after planting, depending on numerous factors. Once mature, the thick trunk of the agave—called the *piña*, for its resemblance to a pineapple—will be separated from the leaves and roots during the harvest, or *jima*.

Opposite page: A worker plants an hijuelo in a rocky field in the Tequila Valley.

AGAVE HARVEST

In the tequila world, nothing is more picturesque than *jimadores* harvesting agave. Tequila brands use these images in their marketing for just that reason. Pictures of a crew of mustachioed, sombrero-clad campesinos whistling along to mariachi as they do battle with acres of spiny foes make for great tequila advertisements, even if in reality the jimadores are more likely to be listening to banda and wearing Dodgers caps.

Jimadores use a specialized tool for blue agave harvesting called the *coa de jima*, or coa for short. It consists of a razor-sharp circular blade affixed to the end of a heavy wooden pole. The jimador begins harvesting each plant by shearing off several pointy leaves (*pencas*) so he can get closer to the heart of the agave. He places his foot up on the open area he's just cut into the agave and puts his weight into the plant to make it lean over. He then uses the coa to hack at the main taproot until it is severed. The severed agave is pushed over onto its side so it can be more safely approached, and the jimador can begin shearing in earnest, eventually removing all the pencas. After one side of the agave is shorn of its pencas, the jimador jabs the coa into it, flips it over, and finishes the other side.

A deft jimador can make harvesting an agave look easy, taking out a big plant in less than a minute. By keeping his coa sharp, striking the agave at a precise angle, and letting gravity help with the work, a jimador conserves energy and works efficiently. Cutting the piña into a smoothly curved ball takes real skill, developed over time. Jimadores average about two minutes per plant, harvesting a couple hundred a day, depending on the weather, terrain, and their age. If an experienced jimador is looking to show off, maybe for tourists or photographers, he can take a plant from living to piña in thirty seconds. But this is dangerous work, and even the most skilled jimador can suffer lost toes or worse.

A harvest crew usually knows which distillery has bought the agave they are harvesting and may customize the jima in small ways. Some

Opposite page: A jimador harvests blue agave with a coa de jima in Tequila, Jalisco.

tequileros have specific parameters about how much penca they want (or will tolerate) left on the piña. While some will accept or even prefer as much as an inch of green penca, others want it *al ras*, that is, shorn as close as possible, with hardly any green cuticle remaining, so that the piña looks like a peeled potato or jícama. Skilled jimadores can customize their harvest of the agave to accommodate such preferences.

The jimadores leave rows of piñas and loose pencas behind them, and a crew of loaders will carry the piñas to a truck, tractor, or burro. The pencas will be left as compost, to be churned into the soil by a tractor later. Mature piñas vary in size, ranging from about 20 pounds to over 150 pounds. Typically, 11 to 12 pounds of raw agave will yield about a liter (1.3 bottles) of tequila. This is a very high yield by weight compared to grain or fruit. After all, the agaves have not been wasting time out in the field for all those years—they were busy converting sunlight, water, and nutrients into carbohydrates that will be converted into tequila!

Once agave is harvested, there is some urgency in getting it to the distillery. If cut agave sits around for more than a day before being processed, precursors of methanol start to form (see The Methanol Bogeyman, page 124). After harvesting, the piñas are loaded onto trucks and taken to the distillery, where they will begin the process of transformation into tequila.

HARVEST TOOLS

COA DE LIMPIEZA
A flat, razor-sharp hoe at the end of a heavy wooden pole. Used for weeding.

CAZANGA
A short-handled scythe used for weeding.

COA DE JIMA
A sharp circular blade at the end of a heavy wooden pole. Used to harvest blue agave.

HYDROLYSIS

At risk of oversimplifying advanced biochemistry, you can think of the heart of the agave as something like a huge yam or potato. Its mass consists primarily of fiber, water, and complex carbohydrates. In the case of agave, these carbs are long, branched molecular chains called fructans. Much like starches, fructan chains are too complex to be easily digested by animals or fermented by yeast. To become edible or fermentable, they must be broken down into smaller, simpler sugars. This process begins naturally as the agave reaches maturity, but it needs help from humans to be at all efficient. In tequila production, complex carbohydrates are converted to sugar in a thermochemical process called hydrolysis. In its simplest form, hydrolysis is the process of steam-cooking the agave. Cooking also breaks down cell walls, softening the plant so that its sweet syrup can be easily extracted when it is crushed or pressed.

The most important product of hydrolysis is sugar, primarily fructose. Sugar is what will ultimately be fermented into alcohol. But agave's biochemical complexity also gives rise to aroma and flavor even at this early stage, as a range of chemical reactions bring forth myriad compounds, including caramels, vanillin, furfurals, terpenes, aldehydes, and even alcohols. Most of these will play a role in how the tequila tastes and smells.

Mesoamerican people began roasting agave hearts in underground pits over 10,000 years ago. While cooked agave was initially a food staple, it was eventually used to make regional mezcals, including the one that evolved into tequila. Over time, roasting gave way to steam cooking—originally in stone ovens and eventually in industrial pressure cookers called autoclaves. Today, all three of these cooking methods (roasting in underground pits, steaming in ovens, and steaming in autoclaves) are used to carry out hydrolysis. In the latter part of the twentieth century, the diffuser, a technology adopted from the sugar industry, was introduced as an efficient yet controversial new method (see The Diffuser Controversy, page 88).

THE AGAVE PRICE ROLLER COASTER

B lue agave has one of the most dramatic price fluctuations of any commodity in the world. For example, the price of agave climbed from a low of 50 Mexican cents in 2006 to a high of 32 pesos per kilo in 2018, an increase of more than 6,000%!

This extreme volatility is exacerbated by the agave's long growing cycle of five to ten years. It works something like this: Agave prices climb as demand for tequila increases. Farmers notice this increase and plant a bunch of agave (often in lieu of staple crops like corn and beans). Each subsequent year, more farmers get in on the action. Five or six years later, when the early birds' agave comes to market, the increase in supply causes agave prices to drop. Farmers then perceive the market softening, and they stop planting new agave. For each of the next few years, as less agave is planted, more is harvested, and the price continues to drop. Twelve or so years after the price peak, when the slowpokes are selling their agave, they may be selling it at a loss—for a lower price than it cost to produce. Once this point is reached, farmers who still have agave in the ground may destroy or abandon their crops.

Left alone, agave will mature, flower, die, and start to rot. Rotting agave is an ideal habitat for picudo weevils and other natural predators. No one is monitoring the abandoned agave, so the bugs have a field day: eating and reproducing in the dying agave, and eventually migrating into neighboring fields en masse to devour healthy plants. Now the supply of agave begins to seriously dwindle. Eventually, supply gets so low that the price rebounds, climbing high enough that farmers can't resist planting, and the whole cycle repeats.

Since 2012, the CRT has made efforts to closely monitor agave supply. But Mexico does not have state agricultural planning, and there are no incentives to plant when demand is slack nor are there subsidies to guarantee a price floor. Farmers and, to a lesser extent, tequila makers bear all of the risk in this volatile price cycle. *Agaveros* are often poor to begin with, and when their timing is off, they become destitute after losing money on an agave crop, especially if they borrowed money to plant their crops. While tequila makers are better off, they certainly can't increase the price of their product anything like sixty times to keep up with agave prices. This creates animosity between agave farmers and tequila makers, which in the early 2000s escalated to an armed standoff in the town of Tequila. Furthermore, the price squeeze at the peak of the cycle encourages less scrupulous, more desperate tequila makers to cut corners to try to cheat the system.

Agave farmers now sell their crops not only to tequila makers but to producers of sweeteners and supplements. This market expansion may ensure that the price of agave never again falls anywhere near a single peso. But there does not appear to be any mutually beneficial plan for farmers and tequila makers on the horizon, so the vicious cycle of agave price fluctuation is likely to continue.

Opposite page: Jimadores harvest blue agave on the property of Tequila Fortaleza (page 168), in Tequila, Jalisco.

STEAM COOKING
STONE OVENS AND AUTOCLAVES

Steam power was introduced to Jalisco in the mid-nineteenth century, and its use became widespread when the railroad arrived in the early twentieth century. Steam cooking rapidly replaced earthen pit roasting because of its greater efficiency and the ability to regulate temperature.

Whether cooking with stone ovens or autoclaves, producers make distinct choices about how to use their equipment. For example, temperature may be maintained at a constant level during cooking or the heat may be turned on and off throughout the cooking process. Many producers prefer to avoid caramelization of agave sugars, which happens at higher temperatures in either cooking method, but others prefer the aroma and flavor notes it produces.

STONE OVENS

Steam-cooking agave in stone ovens, called *hornos de mampostería*, was the standard practice throughout most of the twentieth century, and today it is considered the traditional method by most tequila producers. These relatively crude structures are made from brick, rubble, and cement, with drainage channels in the floor.

Raw agave is stacked inside, generally taking up the entire volume of the oven, from bottom to top and side to side. Ovens may range in size from 15 to 45 tons. The metal door is sealed shut before steam is pumped in through the floor of the oven, resulting in a slight increase above atmospheric pressure.

For two to four hours, the oven isn't yet hot enough to cook the agave, but the steam melts wax from the green cuticle and washes away soil, sap, chlorophyll, and other impurities. This filthy runoff is rather

Opposite page: Cooked agave cools in a stone oven.

euphemistically called "bitter honey" (*mieles amargas*). It is drained through the floor channels to be collected and released as liquid waste. These substances would otherwise ruin the tequila's flavor.

After five to ten more hours, the agave will begin to truly cook. The agaves slowly become darker, sweeter, and softer. The weight of the tons of cooking plant matter begins to crush the piñas on the bottom, pressing out sweet agave syrup (*miel dulce* or *miel de horno*), which eventually rises as high as halfway up the chamber. Like the discarded runoff, this syrup will also be drained through the floor channels, but it will be collected for use in the subsequent steps of formulation and fermentation.

Once the miel has been collected, the drainage channels are again closed, and steam continues to accumulate in the oven until the temperature climbs to around 95°C to 100°C (200°F to 210°F). Cooking time varies among producers, but the process of direct steam infusion generally takes between twenty-four and thirty-six hours. Once the steam is cut, the agaves are left to continue cooking in their own heat, as when a steak is removed from the grill, for another twelve to twenty-four hours. Important chemical reactions that contribute to flavor occur throughout this process. Finally, the oven doors will be opened, allowing the agave to cool enough to be handled.

AUTOCLAVES

Autoclaves are large stainless-steel pressure cookers used to steam-cook agave, potentially much faster than the more traditional brick ovens. (The same technology is used to sterilize instruments in hospitals and tattoo parlors.)

As in the stone oven process, autoclaves cook agave with steam. But by using high pressure, autoclaves significantly reduce cooking time. While some amount of pressure builds up inside stone ovens, autoclaves' hermetically sealed steel doors allow pressure to build up as high as three atmospheres, reducing cooking time to as little as eight

Opposite page: Workers remove cooked agave from an autoclave.

to twelve hours. Autoclaves can also cook at higher temperatures—up to 120°C (250°F). Autoclaves offer more precise control over temperature and pressure than stone ovens and facilitate even cooking of the agave from top to bottom.

While producers who use autoclaves do so mainly for their efficiency, some find a sweet spot with lower pressures and temperatures, cooking more slowly than they could, but still faster than with traditional ovens. Cooking the agave too fast can sacrifice the formation of flavor compounds, so balancing efficiency and quality is an important challenge in autoclave production. Most autoclaves also allow for the separation and drainage of mieles amargas and mieles dulces during the beginning of the cooking.

ROASTING IN EARTHEN PIT OVENS

The original method of cooking agave in earthen pits dates back over 10,000 years. Before the Industrial Revolution, when tequila was still known as vino mezcal de Tequila (mezcal wine from Tequila; see page 18), agave for tequila was cooked the same way it had been cooked for millennia as food and over centuries for producing mezcales. Pit cooking was abandoned for the greater efficiency and yield of steam cooking, but was reintroduced to tequila in 2015, after nearly a century's hiatus.

In earthen (or conical) pit cooking, the oven is a stone-lined hole in the ground, about ten feet (3 m) deep. A bonfire of tree stumps and large logs is ignited at the bottom of the pit. When the fire begins to ebb, its red-hot embers are covered with stones, which will absorb and then release heat. The stones are covered with a layer of damp agave fiber, to avoid charring the bottommost agaves. The rest of the pit is quickly filled with raw agave, which is piled well above ground level, to form something like a diamond-shaped iceberg, with half the mass below ground and half above. The mound of agave is covered with straw mats or tarps and then buried with dirt. The agave will be slowly cooked by the heat of the stones over the course of three to five days. Depending on the type of wood used, the state of the agave, and other factors, the agave will absorb smoky aromas to a greater or lesser degree.

This method of roasting agave for tequila had been retired completely for about a hundred years, until Tequila Cascahuín (page 158) revived the method for several of its tequila labels including Siembra Valles Ancestral and Cascahuín Aniversario. Patrón and Lunazul soon followed suit by making their own products from pit-cooked agave, and José Cuervo has since released a smoke-flavored Maestro

Opposite page, top: Raw agave and an earthen pit oven at Tequila Cascahuín (page 158). *Bottom:* Cooked agave ready to be removed from the pit oven.

Dobel "Humito," inspired by the rising popularity of these ancestral cooking techniques. The use of these methods is expected to increase in the artisanal sector of the industry in coming years, although these tequilas will likely remain specialty products due to their high cost.

DIFFUSERS

In diffuser production, the steps of extraction and hydrolysis are carried out in the reverse of more traditional processes. While earthen pits, brick ovens, and autoclaves extract agave juice after hydrolysis, diffusers are typically used to extract raw agave juice before hydrolyzing it.

The diffusers used for tequila are massive horizontal machines reminiscent of a drive-through car wash for agave. In a "pure diffuser" process, raw agave is shredded mechanically into small pieces that maximize its surface area before being put into the diffuser.

The shredded raw agave is fed onto a porous belt or series of trays. As it moves through the diffuser, the agave is inundated repeatedly with hot (80°C/176°F) water flowing in the opposite direction. The hot water leaches out fructans and other components, then passes through the holes in the belt or trays and is collected in a tank.

The wet fiber that emerges at the other end is pressed dry and by then over 99% of the fructans have been extracted, as they are water-soluble at over 50°C (122°F). The fiber will be discarded, usually to be composted in agave fields.

The extracted liquid is then pumped into vertical autoclaves. There, fructans are converted into simple sugars in a thermal-acid process achieved by adding sulfuric, phosphoric, or hydrochloric acid to the mixture, which lowers the pH and greatly reduces the time necessary for hydrolysis. At least one large producer heats the liquid without the addition of acid, which significantly increases the time needed for hydrolysis. Diffusers are also used in another, "hybrid," way wherein agave is cooked in an autoclave and then fed into a diffuser, which extracts the already simplified sugar from the cooked agave without the use of acids.

Opposite page: Raw agave ready to enter a diffuser (background).

THE DIFFUSER CONTROVERSY

While most tequila drinkers have never heard of a diffuser, it has recently become one of the most divisive topics in the industry. Diffusers are machines used for extraction, usually in conjunction with acid-thermal hydrolysis in an extremely efficient industrial process.

Purists reject any diffuser tequila as chemical-laden industrial junk, produced as cheaply as possible for an ignorant mass market. To diffuser advocates, those critics are no more than privileged snobs who want to keep tequila production primitive so that they can bask in the romantic nostalgia of outdated methods. What's all the fighting about?

The most common way of using a diffuser is to extract raw agave juice and then hydrolyze that juice with acid and heat. The extraction of raw juice from the agave gives some people fits. Tequila was originally a mezcal, and the word "mezcal" comes from the Nahuatl words for "cooked agave." Indeed, cooked agave is one of the primary aromas that tasters look for when evaluating tequilas. Because the whole agave itself

is never cooked in a diffuser process, these tequilas can never truly taste like a "real" tequila, critics contend. In this view, even if the spirit is technically well made, using raw agave juice yields something more like an agave vodka than a true tequila. The neutral flavor of diffuser-extracted, acid-hydrolysis, column-distilled tequilas begs for the maximum use of additives in order to taste like anything at all, critics say.

A second critique of diffusers is that they encourage bad farming practices and pervert the agave market. Because diffuser tequilas are typically distilled to ABVs as high as 80%, then diluted and enhanced with additives, the maturity and complexity of the agave is less important than in traditional processes. Over the years, younger and younger agaves have been harvested for diffuser tequilas, and currently some producers use agave as young as three years old. This rapid turnaround encourages cramming as much agave as possible onto a patch of land and overusing fertilizers and other chemicals. The overall supply of quality, mature agave in the market is thereby reduced. A ceaseless parade of trucks delivers immature agave to the most industrial distilleries, as small artisanal producers struggle to pay for scarce agave and stay in business.

Advocates of the diffuser point out that they get a much higher yield of tequila than traditional producers and thus they claim they are actually contributing to the ultimate sustainability of the industry. Furthermore, they argue that the efficiency and predictability of their process creates consistent, clean products at an accessible price that are among the best-selling tequilas in the world. Their consistency and affordability make them especially attractive as house tequilas for cocktails in high-volume bars and restaurants. These producers are simply meeting the massive global demand for cheap tequila, they say.

Debate about the diffuser often becomes heated and uncivil, and it appears unlikely that partisans on either side can have their minds changed. For baffled consumers stuck in the middle, the best path forward is to learn how tequilas are made, blind-taste as many as possible, and come to their own conclusions based on taste, ethics, and budget.

Opposite page: Shredded raw agave enters a diffuser.

EXTRACTION

In oven or autoclave processes, once the agave's complex carbohydrates have been reduced to simple sugars by cooking, it's time to extract them from the fiber for easier fermentation. To do so, the producer will use a machine to squeeze juice from fiber, using force and pressure.

While a few tequileros continue to ferment with agave fiber in the old style, the vast majority separate the juice and pulp as completely as possible at this stage, discarding the fiber as compost. Extraction is the part of the process that varies the least throughout the industry, but nevertheless it still generates strong opinions among aficionados.

The predominant tool for extracting juice is the roller mill (*molino*), which can be adapted in various ways. A small but increasing number of producers, however, use the more traditional but less efficient *tahona*.

THE ROLLER MILL

Whether large or small, most producers opt for extraction by roller mill. These mechanical presses were developed for the sugar cane industry and adapted for agave. Extraction at a typical tequila distillery is done with a "train" of three to five mills (*tren de molinos*).

Once cooked agave has cooled enough to be handled after coming out of an oven or autoclave, it is passed through a shredder, which tears the agave into fist-sized chunks. A conveyor belt then transports the shredded agave to the first roller mill, which crushes it between three grooved steel spools as it is simultaneously rinsed with water. Both the crushing and the rinsing work to extract sugar from the agave. This process is repeated two to four times as the agave passes through the "train." Each successive mill has narrower grooves in the spool, and each subsequent crush leaves the fiber with less sugar. Agave juice falls into a channel below the mills to be collected in a tank. An optimally adjusted roller mill chain will extract around 96% of sugar from the fiber.

THE TAHONA

Few things in tequila evoke as much nostalgia, romanticism, and awe as tahonas, the two-ton stone wheels that look like they rolled right out of *The Flintstones*. The tahona is a more primitive way of pressing agave juice out of the fiber but it does the same work as a roller mill.

A tahona is a stone wheel attached to an axle that is pulled or pushed around a circular stone pit, crushing cooked agave as it goes. These days, tahonas are generally moved with electric motors, although Tequila Siete Leguas (page 146) has never retired the mule team that pulls its tahona.

With roller mills, agave juice is separated from fiber during each press-and-wash step. Because the tahona works in an enclosed pit, the fiber will begin to reabsorb the extracted juice as soon as the wheel has passed by. It's impossible to extract all of the juice, so there will always be residual sugar left in the fiber. There are two ways to deal with this: fermenting with fiber or adding another rinse.

Before modern plumbing made running water ubiquitous, there was no way to rinse the fiber. Distillers had no choice but to heft the messy stew of liquid, pulp, and wet agave fiber into the fermentation

Opposite page: Cooked agave is pressed and rinsed in a roller mill.

vats all together. Today, a small number of producers, including La Alteña (page 144), Cascahuín (page 158), and Patrón (page 138) still ferment with fiber and other producers rinse the freshly crushed fiber, fermenting only liquid, like in a roller-mill process.

The industry had mostly abandoned the tahona by the 1960s, but La Alteña and Siete Leguas kept the tradition alive. Fortaleza, El Pandillo, and Patrón have all used tahonas since their own launches around the turn of the twenty-first century. As artisanal methods grow in popularity, more producers are beginning to experiment with tahona extraction.

Fans of tahona extraction make many claims about the superiority of this method. However, two facts make it hard to generalize about tahona-produced tequilas. First, out of more than 140 distilleries, around 30 use a tahona for any of their products. That's too small a sample size to extrapolate with much confidence. Furthermore, of those producers, no two are using a tahona in exactly the same way, so it's nearly impossible to draw conclusions.

Workers press cooked agave with a tahona at Tequila Fortaleza (page 168).

Why do tahona tequilas engender such intense loyalty? Some of it is doubtlessly owing to nostalgia and respect for tradition. But the tequilas produced using tahonas do tend to be of remarkable quality, making it hard to question the process. Regardless of any specific effects that tahona extraction has on flavor, its use indicates a tolerance for lower efficiencies and yields. Producers who are willing to make that sacrifice are probably also taking great care with the rest of their process: using healthy, mature agave and cooking it rather than using acid hydrolysis (see Diffusers, page 87), allowing natural fermentation the time it needs, and distilling with an eye toward flavor. Tahona extraction is a signifier of a tangible commitment to a "craft" process where efficiency is sacrificed for quality.

FORMULATION

Formulation is a small but crucial step in the tequila production process. In formulation, the sweet juice extracted from the cooked agave is brought to the optimal percentage of sugar for fermentation.

In tequila production, the ideal sugar level for fermentation is 4% to 5%. Cooked juice from healthy, mature agave is more than 20% sugar, far more than most yeast can handle, so when it's time to begin fermentation, the juice is diluted with water, turning it into aguamiel and making it more easily fermentable. In rarer cases where the agave has less sugar than expected or the juice is overly diluted, miel de horno (the first syrup reserved during the cooking process) can be added during formulation to raise the sugar content.

Formulation is also where "other sugars" are added in the production of a mixto tequila (see Two Categories of Tequila, page 50). In effect, the volume of aguamiel to be fermented is doubled with the addition of sugar and water at this stage. This helps to explain the great difference in price between 100% agave and other tequilas.

MYTH OF THE
MASTER DISTILLER

The figure of the master distiller looms large in contemporary tequila lore. In the aficionado's imagination, a lone genius (male, mustachioed, wearing a brimmed hat) stands before an alembic still, carefully eyeing the steady flow of tequila emerging from the serpentine and using his senses of smell and taste to make the "cuts" at precisely the right moment.

These days, producing tequila is a team effort, and the idea of a single master distiller is a bit of a myth. A tequila's profile is established in part through sensory perception and tasting, but it is also almost always created with the input of a chemist or chemical engineer who can connect aromas in the glass with specific compounds that show up in lab analysis. This approach establishes certain parameters within which cuts should be made in distillation (see page 106). The physical act of making cuts is generally performed by an experienced, skilled distillery employee—not the brand owner, who is often publicly regarded as the master distiller.

Distilling enough tequila to meet global demand is certainly no longer a one-person job, even in the smallest distilleries. But the brand or distillery owner is often extremely knowledgeable about the entire process, and some of them certainly could distill tequila on their own if they had to. At the end of the day, it is their name and reputation that is associated with the tequila's quality, whether they are physically pulling levers or not.

FERMENTATION

After agave juice is hydrolyzed, extracted, and formulated, it's ready to ferment. Fermentation is a biochemical process in which microbes convert a carbohydrate into an alcohol or an acid. In tequila making, yeast converts the sugars extracted from agave into ethyl alcohol, a.k.a. ethanol. However, this process also yields small amounts of other compounds that have an important role in defining a tequila's flavor profile. These compounds—commonly called "congeners"—are what give tequila its complexity of aroma and flavor. More than 200 distinct congeners may be found in any single tequila.

While tequila is limited to a single varietal of agave as raw material, the blue agave's biochemical complexity results in remarkable organoleptic, or sensorial, complexity. In fact, agave spirits (i.e., mezcal and tequila) are the most chemically and aromatically complex white (unaged) distillates in the world. The birth of flavor in tequila begins with hydrolysis, but the perceivable flavors at that stage are relatively basic compared to what's next. Cooked blue agave is undeniably delicious, but it's also relatively plain, often described as sweet, vegetal, earthy, "yammy," and "prunish." Nearly all other aromas and flavors in a blanco tequila are formed in fermentation. The panoply of fruit, spice, herb, and floral notes simply do not exist before the fermentation stage.

The scientific knowledge of fermentation is barely over 120 years old, and a lot of mystery remains to be explored in this part of the tequila production process. Processes that are well understood under laboratory conditions are far less clear in functioning distilleries, especially those that have inherited pre-scientific traditions. We don't know the exact microbial makeup inside any given distillery; the precise role played by nearby trees, livestock, and insects; or how the interplay between yeast, bacteria, and temperature specifically impacts flavor. All this lends a certain sense of magic to this crucial step.

ELEMENTS OF FERMENTATION

Fermentation is simple in its broad strokes and complex at the level of fine detail. It's easy to get lost in those details. But to appreciate the importance of fermentation in tequila production, it is crucial to understand three basic elements: yeast, ethanol, and congeners.

YEAST + SUGAR → ALCOHOL + FLAVOR

 YEAST. Yeast are microscopic single-celled fungi. These tiny workhorses turn simple sugars into the ethanol in tequila. Yeast are around us at all times. More than 1,500 species of yeast have been identified, and scientists estimate there are likely more than 400 times this many yet to be found in nature. As is the case with humans, there is an incredible range of genetic diversity within single species of yeast, as they have evolved in geographically specific populations. The combination of yeast's genetic diversity and the agave's biochemical complexity is what makes tequila so interesting and tasty.

The dominant yeast species in beverage alcohol production is *Saccharomyces cerevisiae*. It is one of the most-studied microbes on the planet, and it does the heavy lifting in terms of ethanol production. Even though it is the best-known yeast species, biologists still understand the function of only half of its genes—and even less is understood about the dozen other yeasts that have been identified in the distinct phases of tequila's fermentation.

The specific genetic strain of each yeast varies from distillery to distillery and ultimately functions in particular ways to synthesize compounds that drinkers will perceive as aroma and flavor. No two distilleries have the same microbial environment, and this makes it impossible to move a tequila brand from one distillery to another without a noticeable change in flavor profile.

ETHANOL. Ethanol—the only alcohol humans can drink much of—is made from sugar by yeast. We classify alcoholic beverages based on their raw material, or sugar source: Fermented fruit juice is called wine; malted and fermented grain is called beer. Distill the former, and you have brandy, schnapps, or eau-de-vie. The latter likewise can yield whiskey, vodka, or gin, depending on what you do with it. In other words, not all sugar sources are created equal. While pure sugar (e.g., fructose, sucrose, or glucose) is pure sugar, in nature these sugars come in various "packages" (e.g., fruit, grain, agave) that contain other compounds that may both complicate and enrich fermentation. Likewise, ethanol is ethanol, whether it's in whiskey, vodka, or tequila, but it is the other compounds formed alongside ethanol in fermentation that give each drink its unique character.

 **CONGENERS.** "Congener" is the generic term used for volatile, organoleptic compounds formed in fermentation along with ethanol. Ethanol is what gives you a buzz, regardless of its sugar source. Congeners are what make tequila taste like tequila, rum taste like rum, and so on.

In tequila, the most important classes of congeners are superior alcohols, esters, and aldehydes. All three are potentially toxic, and therefore are regulated by the Norm (see page 50). All three are also vital to tequila's aroma, flavor, and structure. For example, high levels of superior alcohols are what make some tequilas taste "hot" or overly alcoholic, even at low ABV.

Esters arguably contribute tequila's most important "secondary" aromas—those that do not come directly from the cooked agave. Without them, a lot of flavor would be lost. The most common examples of fruit, floral, and spice aromas come from various esters in tequila, including citrus blossom, apple, anise, banana, and honey.

The most common aldehyde in tequila—acetaldehyde—is another naturally formed by-product of fermentation. At low concentrations, aldehydes give off a range of pleasant aromas, used in perfumes. At least eight different aldehydes are found in tequila, including vanillin.

While the primary goal of fermentation is ethanol production, congeners are far from mere by-products. They are crucial to making a beverage that is interesting, distinct, and flavorful. The unique balance struck between all these elements during fermentation forms the palette that the distiller has to work with in the following phase of distillation.

YEAST AS TERROIR

Foods and beverages with Geographical Indication status, like tequila, are supposed to exhibit terroir, which is colloquially understood as "the taste of a place." The idea that the profiles of tequila from the Valley are distinct from those from the Highlands has long been debated. In a general way, Tequila Ocho has settled the question as to whether agave provenance can make a difference in flavor: It can (see page 164).

The maturity, health, and carbohydrate content of agave is paramount to the quality and complexity of any tequila, and the soil, elevation, and microclimate where the agave is grown will be determinative of those factors. These factors are commonly considered in discussing a tequila's terroir.

However, terroir expresses the totality of production factors—natural and human—that go into making a product like tequila. While often overlooked, yeast is one of those factors. The various strains of yeast that thrive in a distillery evolved in that location, and they are not found in exactly the same form anywhere else. That is the very meaning of terroir! Yeast, whether deftly manipulated or simply allowed to do its thing, is as important as agave to a tequila's flavor profile.

Opposite page: Various stages of fermentation in open stainless-steel vats.

THE FERMENTATION PROCESS IN TEQUILA

Fermentation in tequila varies from inarguably industrial to completely spontaneous. The basics, however, are the same in every process.

Most producers use a proprietary strain of *Saccharomyces cerevisiae* yeast—either one they isolated from their own distillery or one purchased from a commercial lab. A tiny number of producers do not add any yeast at all, but simply allow the ambient microbes in the distillery to work their biochemical magic.

Basically, yeast do two things: They reproduce, and they eat. A tequilero can control which thing the yeast does by manipulating the relative amounts of available oxygen and sugar.

At first, it's important that the yeast reproduce to create a large enough population to ferment efficiently. The producer makes this happen by feeding a small amount of aguamiel to a small amount of yeast, with plenty of air around. In the presence of lots of oxygen and a little sugar, aerobic fermentation begins. The yeast are not really fermenting much at this stage, but they're reproducing exponentially, splitting themselves into new cells over and over.

When there is enough yeast, the tequilero will move the yeast-aguamiel solution into a larger vat and pump in hundreds more liters of sugary aguamiel. Now, with way more sugar and less oxygen in the bigger tank, the yeast start the big show: anaerobic fermentation and the production of ethanol and congeners.

Thermal energy (heat) and carbon dioxide (CO_2) gas are by-products of fermentation. During fermentation, CO_2 gas slowly begins to emerge as tiny bubbles rising to the surface of the fermenter. After about a day, the fermenting liquid (called *mosto*, or "must") can look like it is boiling, as a steady flow of larger CO_2 bubbles rise to the surface and burst. This active-looking liquid is now called *mosto vivo* ("living must").

Aromas will change perceptibly over the course of fermentation, with alcohols being formed near the beginning of the process and esters toward the end. In general, the mosto will evolve from sweet to bitter

Opposite page: Actively fermenting mosto vivo with fiber.

over time. Open-top fermentation generally takes between three to six days, varying by season as the ambient temperature changes.

Saccharomyces cerevisiae is a bit of a Goldilocks. It has a distinct comfort zone in terms of temperature, pH, sugar level, and nutrient availability. Too much or too little of any element can kill the yeast or otherwise arrest fermentation. Eventually, the yeast will have consumed most of the available sugar as well as produced enough ethanol to make their environment unlivable. Having served admirably, the yeast die, and their remains sink to the bottom of the vat and join the other solids that will be left behind in distillation.

In less controlled processes, ambient bacteria may also carry out a secondary, malolactic fermentation. Malolactic fermentation produces organic acids (especially lactic acid) rather than alcohols and typically occurs once the yeast have finished primary fermentation. While bacterial fermentation is avoided by many producers, some enjoy the lactic notes that it can impart—aromas that range from sweet cream and butterscotch to ripe, funky cheese.

Once all fermentation is complete, the resulting liquid, now akin to an agave beer, is called *mosto muerto* ("dead must"). This is what will be distilled to produce tequila.

VARIATIONS IN TEQUILA FERMENTATION

At the industrial end of the spectrum, producers use massive fermentation vats with capacities of 100,000 liters or more. They may be sealed and use efficient commercial yeast with added nutrients that facilitate faster fermentation. This type of fermentation can convert sugar into alcohol in less than twenty-four hours. This process achieves maximum alcohol production in minimum time, but sacrifices flavor complexity.

Only the most industrial distilleries ferment in sealed containers. Most of the industry ferments in open-top vats, some as small as 2,000 liters. Open, slower fermentation in a rich microbial environment yields more flavor than sealed, highly efficient fermentation.

A small but growing number of producers harken to tradition by fermenting the aguamiel with agave fiber (*bagazo*) from the extraction process. Fermenting with fiber lends robust flavor to the final product, but this traditional practice sacrifices efficiencies for organoleptic benefits.

The most common fermenter material is stainless steel. A few micro-producers use wooden vats or tile-lined tanks made of concrete or fiberglass. Fermenter material doesn't have an appreciable impact on flavor, but the latter materials have advantages when it comes to insulation. Both wood and tile fermenters maintain fairly stable temperatures, regardless of the season. The temperature of stainless steel vats can fluctuate in ways that can be challenging for fermentation.

For example, in the torrid Tequila Valley summer, producers may run a water drip down the sides of steel vats to keep them cool enough for fermentation to continue. In the Highlands, they have the opposite problem. Some producers there run steam through steel coils at the bottom of their tanks to raise the temperature.

Seasonal differences in temperature will result in variations in flavor profiles. These can be embraced and made part of the brand's small-batch identity or tempered through blending distinct batches, filtration, or additives for greater consistency.

STILL MATERIAL

Both column and alembic stills may be made of copper, stainless steel, or a combination of the two. Most tequila stills are made mainly of stainless steel. Stainless has the virtues of lower cost, greater longevity, and ease of cleaning. While full copper stills are increasingly rare, they have important virtues as well.

Copper was the material of choice for centuries. Copper is now far more expensive than stainless steel, and it corrodes over time, requiring regular maintenance. While there is nostalgia for copper stills, there is also an important scientific reason why copper is preferred by many. Distillation doesn't add anything; it only takes away. In the case of copper, this is true in a particularly important way. Why does copper corrode or break down? Copper binds with sulfur compounds in the mosto and pulls them out of solution. Sulfur is universally unappealing to humans, so using copper has an inarguably positive effect on flavor profiles. What we can describe as loss to the still can be seen as a type of purification of the eventual tequila.

These days, many producers opt for hybrid stills, wherein most of the body is stainless steel, but the heating coil or other interior components are copper. This provides some of the benefits of both materials.

DISTILLATION

If fermentation tends toward magic, distillation approaches art. Nature plays a large role in both agave farming and in fermentation. But at the distillation stage, humans are calling the shots, and the distiller has more control over the process. No two distillers work in quite the same way, so there is room for each one to leave an imprint of artistry and personality on their tequila.

At its core, distillation uses heat to separate alcohol from water. In its details, there is quite a bit more going on. All of the flavor that will be present in blanco tequila is already there before distillation; it's simply trapped among a bunch of other elements. Distillation frees the flavors.

Before being distilled, the mosto muerto created from fermentation bears little resemblance to a pristine blanco tequila in appearance or flavor: It looks like an opaque broth. But at the molecular level, it is composed of scores of distinct chemical elements that were formed during the processes of hydrolysis and fermentation. Distillation does not add anything to this mélange of flavor and potential intoxication. Instead, distillation is a process of separating what we don't want from what we do want and concentrating the good stuff.

In tequila, there are two basic ways to do this: discontinuous distillation in pot (or alembic) stills, or continuous distillation in columns.

THE BASICS OF POT DISTILLATION

Most tequileros distill in pot or alembic stills. This method is also called discontinuous distilling because the still must be emptied and cleaned between each batch. An alembic still consists of several parts. The large tank, or pot, at its base contains a heating coil. The pot is sealed at the top by the *capitel*, which looks like an upside-down funnel. A large curved tube at the top of the capitel, called the gooseneck, connects the capitel to the condenser.

After fermentation, the mosto muerto is pumped into the pot to be heated by the steam-filled coil. Each chemical compound in the mosto has a unique boiling point. As the distiller slowly raises the temperature of the liquid, these compounds begin to evaporate ("boil off"), one after another, forming a gaseous continuum—or parade—of different compounds, which will be captured at the end of the process.

As the temperature increases, the lightest, most volatile compounds evaporate, followed by the next lightest, and on down the line to the heaviest of the compounds. This steam train of chemical compounds rises up through the capitel and continues into the gooseneck. From there, it passes into the condenser and flows into a tube that is submerged in cold running water. The sudden drop in temperature converts the compounds from vapor back into liquid. They trickle down the pipe, maintaining the same chemical order in which they vaporized.

The liquid flows out of a spigot at the bottom of the condenser. There stands the distiller, who has been carefully measuring the temperature of the pot, the time that has passed, and the percentage of ethanol in the liquid flowing from the condenser, waiting to "cut" the distillate at just the right time. Since ethanol is among the lightest compounds in the mosto muerto, the percentage of ethanol starts high and drops over time, approaching zero. As the liquid emerges from the condenser, the distiller physically separates the distillate into three parts: the heads, the body (or heart), and the tails. The timing of those "cuts" depends on the level of ethanol emerging from the condenser, and it is crucial to the final product.

The initial part of the flow is considered the "heads." In tequila, the heads are high in both alcohol and flavor. But they contain some potentially harmful compounds too, like superior alcohols. The heads are collected in a "heads and tails" container. When the distiller decides it is time to "cut" the heads, they throw a lever and divert the flow of liquid into a tank, where the "heart" of the batch is amassed. What flows for the next few hours is the good stuff. Alcohol and flavor are initially both quite high in the emerging liquid, but as time passes, the alcohol content of the heart will continue to drop. The flavors will vary with time, too—passing, perhaps, from fruity to floral to spicy and edging toward nutty, creamy, and lactic toward the end. After a few hours, the distiller decides when it's time to make the "tails cut." The lever will be returned to its original position, diverting the flow of tails to the smaller container, where they

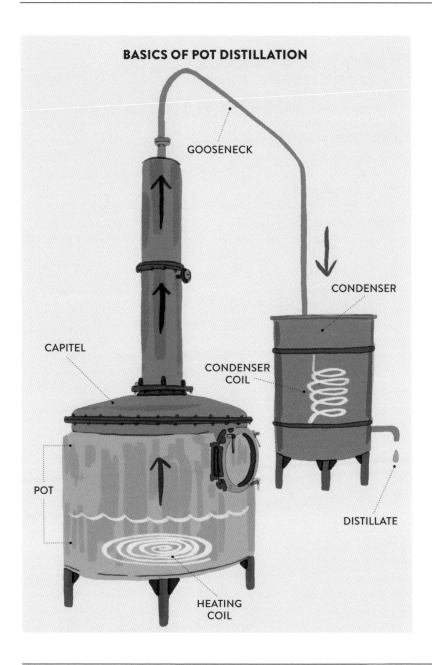

BASICS OF POT DISTILLATION

GOOSENECK

CONDENSER

CONDENSER
COIL

CAPITEL

POT

DISTILLATE

HEATING
COIL

DISTILLING BACKWARD: AZEOTROPES IN TEQUILA

Tequila is complex. Details that are straightforward in other spirits become complicated with tequila. For example, methanol is lighter than ethanol, which is lighter than water. So, on paper, when the fermented liquid in a still is heated, methanol should vaporize first—in the heads—followed by ethanol, and finally trailed by water. This is what happens in most other spirits.

Distillers from other traditions are dumbfounded when they learn that in agave spirits, methanol is spread throughout the flow of distillation and concentrated in the tails. Compared to every other spirit, tequila "distills backward," in a sense.

This happens because of azeotropes. An azeotrope is a mixture of two liquids, bound together by strong molecular attraction. Because of this strong bond, they boil together at a temperature that may be above or below the normal boiling point of either compound.

In the mosto muerto created by fermentation of agave juice, some of the methanol and ethanol combine into azeotropes. Some methanol acts "normally" and boils off in the heads. A bit of it continues to evaporate with ethanol throughout the distillation, before finally peaking near the end. A competent distiller makes the tails cut before that peak occurs.

This phenomenon is more than just a scientific oddity. It means that compared to distillers of other spirits, tequileros have more freedom to play with the heads, since they are relatively lower in methanol. The heads are where a ton of aroma and flavor hang out, so this "backward" aspect of tequila production is part of what makes it one of the world's most complex distilled spirits.

mix with the heads. The tails are mostly water and other heavier elements, but they also contain high levels of methanol and smell unpleasant. For many distillers, the combined heads and tails are now waste, to be treated and discarded as stillage, or *vinazas*. But because of the imprecise nature of pot distilling, there is still ethanol in the heads and (to a lesser extent) in the tails, so some distillers choose to add the heads, tails, or both to the next batch of mosto muerto to be re-distilled.

In a pot distillation process, tequila will be distilled at least twice to reach the 35% ABV minimum required by the Norm. The first distillation is called *destrozamiento* (destroying) and it produces *ordinario*, or "ordinary." Ordinary is about 20% to 25% ABV. It is often milky in appearance, and can taste anywhere from unpleasant to something like a diluted "tequila cooler." The second distillation is called rectification, and converts the ordinary into tequila, usually with an ABV of 45% to 60%. Tequila must be 35% to 55% ABV at the time of bottling, so this "still-strength" tequila will be either diluted, filtered, and bottled as blanco, or stored in wood for maturation and aging.

THE COMPLEXITIES OF POT DISTILLATION

In practice, the process of distillation is more chaotic and unpredictable than the simplified explanation above. Inside of a pot still, compounds are boiling, atomizing, evaporating, recondensing, and breaking chemical bonds based on factors like the ambient temperature, the shape of the still, and how those two elements interact to create different surface temperatures on different parts of the still. Tequila stills often have expansion chambers, reflux devices, and other components whose technical purpose and function are often unknown to the distillers themselves. The form of the still is usually inherited from a previous generation or copied from a neighbor. There is a fine line between tradition and superstition in distillation. With so many unknowns, the neat, orderly steps described above will rarely match the reality of pot distillation. It's as if the painter's palette, the sculptor's stone, or the composer's very notes were never quite where she expected them to be. That margin of error, that zone of mystery, is intrinsic to this artistic medium.

Art or not, every batch of tequila will have to pass muster at the CRT's labs. The esters, aldehydes, and superior alcohols limited by the Norm and measured at the lab are all crucial for aroma and flavor. Distillation is the last chance to balance potential flavor against potential toxicity. Even within the strict parameters of the Norm, there is ample room for individual expression in distillation. If four distillers are each assigned a different vat of mosto in the same distillery, they could make minutely different cuts of heads and tails and produce four distinct tequilas. No manual specifies where the heads, heart, and tails begin and end. The precise moment the cuts are made can be the difference between a fruity, floral, spicy, or neutral tequila. Some distillers will make very small cuts in the first distillation, and a few don't cut heads at all. Others filter the ordinario before the second distillation. In these moments, distillation becomes art. A distiller takes raw material, works within established parameters, and makes choices that will result in a tequila that expresses their taste and vision.

COLUMN DISTILLATION

While pot distillation is used in most distilleries, the largest volumes of tequila are produced in column stills. Also called continuous distillation, this method is similar to the technology used to refine oil. A distillation column houses dozens of copper plates, arrayed along the height of the column. At each plate, evaporation and condensation occur. This allows the distiller to precisely isolate the various compounds spread out along the continuum of vapors and pull them out in a pure form. A single pass through a column could just as accurately be described as either a single distillation or several simultaneous distillations because microdistillations are happening at each plate.

Column stills offer the possibility of both greater control over distillation and higher levels of purity. But because distillation refines alcohol, there is a risk of neutering the spirit to the point where it isn't interesting to drink. While it is possible to distill to 96% pure ethanol using a column still, it would defeat the purpose of using agave, whose high cost can only be justified by its unique flavors. In spirits, "impurities" are synonymous with aroma and flavor—both good and bad.

Column stills are designed for efficiency, but a producer interested in quality can make trade-offs to benefit from those efficiencies, without sacrificing much quality and flavor.

Opposite page: A copper and stainless-steel column still at the La Tequileña distillery (page 160).

AGING TEQUILA

The end result of distillation is tequila—at last! At root, tequila is a white spirit, and most tequila is consumed in its silver, unaged form. This has always been the case. No other white spirit can compete with the agave's complexity of aroma and flavor. Nevertheless, people love aged tequilas, too. Reposados, añejos, and extra-añejos are the most amicable points of entry for lovers of whiskey and other aged spirits. Toasted or charred oak can impart strong notes of vanilla, caramel, and chocolate, flavors that most people find appealing. Time in the barrel also allows the tequila to come into balance, losing some of the sharper notes associated with blancos.

AGING IN OAK

Tequila can be legally aged in any kind of oak—American oak, French oak, or the more exotic European oaks. The type of oak and barrel affects both flavor profile and price. In practice, the vast majority of aged tequila spends time in used American whiskey barrels. Used French oak barrels are the next most common aging vessel.

Bourbon whiskey must be aged in unused, charred American oak barrels. The barrels are sold to producers of other spirits after a single use. French oak barrels are made mostly for wine and brandies and are considerably more expensive than American oak. The use of French oak (both used and new) in tequila is still relatively novel but is becoming increasingly common. Diversifying barrel types is an easy way for tequila brands to distinguish themselves in a crowded marketplace.

American oak tends to impart vanilla and sweet, buttery notes. French oak is known for spice notes and higher tannins, leading to a drier mouthfeel. American oak's looser wood grain means that flavor is infused faster than with French oak, where slower aging can allow for closer monitoring of the change in flavors over time.

WHAT'S THE BARREL DO?

Barrel aging simultaneously gives, takes away, and masks flavor as it infuses, filters, and mellows the tequila inside. The most obvious result is the transfer of color, aroma, and flavor from the wood. As the surrounding temperature changes from day to night and from season to season, the wood fibers expand and contract as the tequila cyclically seeps in and out of the charred oak. This process is a bit like making tea: The color and flavor of the tea leaves steep into the surrounding hot water. The longer the soak, the stronger the tea and the less residual color and flavor is left in the teabag. Similarly, a newly charred barrel quickly imparts strong doses of color and flavor. Every time the barrel is filled, it has a little bit less to give, and it changes the liquid less, as happens when reusing a tea bag. Barrels, however, can be re-charred multiple times.

Barrels also facilitate a less obvious process of filtration. Charring the inside of a barrel creates a layer of charcoal that lines the entire interior surface of the barrel. Like a piece of burnt firewood, this charcoal layer is cracked and rutted. These cracks increase the amount of surface area that comes into contact with the tequila as it seeps in and out of them, so aging occurs faster than in more lightly toasted barrels. The charcoal also filters out esters and other impurities. But one person's impurities are another's flavor, and this is one reason for the sharp division between tequila drinkers who prefer blancos and those who prefer aged tequilas.

After distillation, the tequila settles, or comes into balance through slow chemical processes that would occur even without the influence of the barrel. But the chemical composition of the wood itself may facilitate those reactions, and the porosity of oak allows for a slow exchange of gases through the barrel. Oxygen dissolves into the tequila over time, contributing to a smoother, rounder mouthfeel.

All these factors contribute to the softening, mellowing, and (sometimes) sweetening of blanco tequila into reposado, añejo, or extra-añejo. Whether that is an improvement or not depends upon individual taste.

RESTING WITHOUT OAK

Some consider freshly distilled blanco tequila to be a real treat, but it is too harsh for most palates. Time and contact with oxygen mellows and balances a blanco's sharper notes. Resting tequila in sealed glass damajuanas (demijohns) was the norm before the use of oak barrels became common, and it is still done in mezcal-producing regions today. These days, most tequila distillers rest their blanco in sealed stainless-steel containers for days or weeks after distillation. This process can be hurried along by bubbling air or pure oxygen through the resting tequila. Meanwhile, Cascahuín (page 158) and a few other distilleries have begun experimenting with bringing back the traditional practice of resting in glass.

BLENDING AND SINGLE BARRELS

While the hundreds of barrels in a barrel house may look the same, they aren't. The regions, trees, and staves that gave birth to each barrel differ, leading to subtle flavor differences. Even the barrel's position in the barrel house—close to the cool floor or tepid ceiling, near an open door, or in the middle of a row with less airflow—has huge effects on the intensity of flavors that form during aging.

Unless labeled otherwise, a bottle of aged tequila is a blend of dozens or even hundreds of different barrels, just as in whiskey or wine. While different barrel types can be mixed and matched for tequila blends and the same tequila can pass through different barrel types, barrel blending is a delicate art that allows a producer to maintain a consistent flavor profile even as batches of blanco vary somewhat and the intensity imparted by the barrels declines over time. With each subsequent filling, or "posture," a barrel has a bit less flavor, aroma, and color to give to tequila the next time around. To correct for that, tequileros can create blends with larger quantities of tequila aged in fresher barrels each time, or they leave tequila in the "tired" barrels for more time before adding it to the blend.

Following whiskey trends, single-barrel tequilas are becoming increasingly popular. Single barrels are just what they sound like: The contents of a single barrel are bottled and labeled, distinguished from all other tequilas with a unique barrel number or memorable name. Choosing among different barrels allows producers or their clients to emphasize particular organoleptic elements that would otherwise be subdued or hidden in a commercial blend. As completely unique products, single-barrel tequilas are quick sellers with collectors seeking to outdo each other with exclusive acquisitions.

Opposite page: Blanco tequila rests in glass carboys sealed with corncobs at Tequila Cascahuín (page 158).

IS AGED
TEQUILA BETTER?

Every class of tequila can be delicious. Seasoned aficionados appreciate all five classes (see The Five Classes of Tequila, page 52) even if their personal preferences tend toward a particular one. That said, aged tequila is more accessible to the palates of North Americans and others coming from whiskey cultures. In English-speaking countries, brown spirits have always been considered the finest, so many people assume aged tequila is superior to blanco. And the longer tequila spends in a whiskey barrel, the more it will have in common with whiskey. So aged tequilas typically speak to the palates of whiskey drinkers more fluently than blancos. For the same reason, purists and people from other cultures may find that barrel aging blunts the most interesting complexities of blanco tequila, making it less unique and more whiskey-like over time. It's all a matter of subjective preference, and the key is to develop a discerning palate that can evaluate and appreciate all classes of tequila.

However, do not make the common mistakes of assuming that the color of a tequila tells you about its aging or that a higher price indicates greater quality. In general, you'd expect tequilas to be darker the longer they have been barrel aged. In reality, the char or toast level of the barrel and the number of times the barrel has been used since charring also significantly influence the tequila's hue. What's more, the use of caramel coloring and oak extract (permitted for use as additives; see page 52) can add color and emulate other aspects of aging that are not apparent to the naked eye but are detectable to trained tasters. At the other extreme, there are additive-free tequilas, aged in "tired" barrels that have seen multiple postures, in which the color difference between reposado and añejo is barely detectable. Purists tend to prefer the latter tequilas, where the influence of the blanco slowly diminishes with time in the barrel, rather than being immediately erased by more aggressive aging.

The higher price of aged tequilas does not indicate an inherent increase in quality but rather compensates for a loss in product. During aging, some of the product is absorbed by the barrel and lost to evaporation. In whiskey production, this is the famous "angel's share"; in tequila it is known as *merma*. In the arid environment of Jalisco, it's possible to lose as much as 10% of a barrel's volume annually. Fans of añejos and extra-añejos must pay not only for the tequila in the bottle but for the tequila that was lost to the environment—or to the angels.

Tequila ages in used American whiskey barrels at Tequila Arette (page 162).

FINISHING TOUCHES: DILUTION, FILTRATION, AND BOTTLING

Dilution, filtration, and bottling are the final steps in producing tequila for sale. While easy to overlook, there are important details at these steps in making tequila that can have major effects on the final product.

DILUTION

When newly distilled, tequila may have an ABV exceeding the legal limit of 55%. Aged tequila will typically lose ABV in the barrel, but under certain ambient conditions, it may instead lose water and increase its ABV. In any case, the high alcohol content of freshly distilled tequila ensures that almost all tequila will be diluted with water. The vast majority of tequila is sold at 38% to 40% ABV, so most distillers are adding quite a bit of water to their finished product before it hits the market. If your bottle of tequila is 40% ABV, given the small concentrations of congeners present, well over half of what you are drinking is water. That means the source and quality of that water make a huge difference in the quality of the beverage. Most producers use either distilled or deionized/demineralized water. While these processes purify the water to a certain extent, the differences in flavor, salinity, and especially mouthfeel vary greatly among these different processes. Smaller producers may use spring, well, or even rainwater to dilute, which adds to the unique character of their tequilas.

Diluting tequila is much more complicated than, say, making Kool-Aid: You don't just haphazardly mix the two ingredients together. As in nearly every other part of the tequila production process, dilution involves physiochemical changes at the molecular level. New chemical

Opposite page: Sergio Mendoza blends tequila samples in the lab at the La Tequileña distillery (page 160).

WHAT'S SO BAD ABOUT FATTY ACIDS?

Fatty acids are a natural consequence of tequila production and were never a problem until large volumes of tequila were exported to cold climates outside of Mexico. In these regions, lipids like fatty acids solidify. In a bottle of tequila, they can form "clouds," haze, or even chunks. While these solids quickly dissipate when the bottle is shaken, no brand wanted to be the only cloudy tequila on the shelf in Vancouver, Oslo, or Moscow, so almost everyone began chill filtering their tequila. In chill filtering, the tequila's temperature is lowered to filter out fatty acids. At lower temperatures, the fatty acids—natural components of the agave—solidify and fall out of solution and are trapped by the filters, allowing the rest of the cold liquid to pass through. The problem with this practice is that fatty acids provide a lot of agave flavor and pleasant mouthfeel. In fact, the oily residue left behind on cellulose filters in a chiller process is extremely aromatic—something like agave butter. The vast difference between the filtered and unfiltered versions of the same batch of tequila is evident to even the most inexperienced tasters in blind tastings. Bolder, unfiltered tequilas can certainly be challenging to novice palates and are not universally preferred. But tequila aficionados are increasingly on the lookout for less-filtered and unfiltered tequilas, clouds or no clouds.

bonds are formed when water and tequila are mixed, and existing molecules arrange themselves into different shapes, changing factors like the viscosity of the liquid. A good blender will dilute carefully over time, allowing the mixture to settle as it goes, rather than chaotically sloshing everything together at once.

DILUTION OF AGED TEQUILA

There are two ways to handle dilution of aged tequilas: before and after barreling. The methods are completely opposite but each has a coherent logic and each is capable of leading to lovely tequilas in the right hands. The most common way to dilute aged tequila is to barrel age still-strength blanco, and then dilute the aged tequila prior to filtration and bottling. This is the most efficient use of barrel space, although the subsequently diluted tequila will need to be allowed to settle, rest, and oxygenate as the tequila and water slowly wed.

On the other hand, a smaller number of producers dilute their aged tequila *before* barreling it. The logic here is that if the water is aged along with the tequila, there will be a more coherent and complete merging of liquids and flavors. The tequilero can also make a relatively accurate calculation of how much water to add so that when the liquid is extracted, it's as close to bottling proof as possible.

FILTRATION

Almost all tequila is filtered prior to bottling, although there is a movement afoot toward lighter filtration or none at all, especially for specialty products. The most basic filtration involves passing tequila through thin paper filters under low pressure. This removes particulate matter, which is especially important for aged tequilas that have been drained from charred barrels.

At the other extreme, filtration with activated carbon (essentially charcoal) aggressively removes impurities—impurities that include aroma, flavor, and color. Overdone, charcoal filtration may neuter an excellent tequila to the point of having no character. This is sometimes the intent, an attempt to "dumb down" tequila for the mass market. The most aggressive charcoal filtration is used to produce "cristalino" tequila (see page 61). Most tequileros operate between those two extremes, using an accordion-like series of cellulose filters whose quantity and thickness can be adjusted.

BOTTLING AND LABELING

B ottling and labeling are the final steps in making tequila, and both are regulated by the CRT. Tequila can be bottled in glass, ceramic, or food-grade plastic. The maximum vessel size is 5 liters, and plastic jugs of that size are commonly sold on the roadside in and around the Tequila Valley. Other countries may have smaller maximum sizes. For example, 1.75-liter and 2-liter bottles are the largest sizes allowed in the United States and European Union, respectively. All 100% agave tequila must be bottled within the Denomination of Origin for Tequila (DOT) region. Mixto tequila can be bottled anywhere in the world with the authorization of the CRT, an allowance that is widely critiqued (see Two Categories of Tequila, page 50).

A surprising amount of tequila is still bottled by hand, given Mexico's low wages and the high cost of importing state-of-the-art bottling machines. Either way, bottles are generally rinsed out with tequila to clean and sterilize them before filling.

Labels for all exported tequila are required to display the category and class of the tequila, the brand name, the official NOM and CRT logos, the four-digit number of the producer responsible for the tequila, some version of "Made in México," and the batch or lot number. The lot number may be prominently displayed as part of the brand's identity or machine-printed in tiny type on the inside of the label, making it difficult to see. Using that number, the CRT should be able to trace the origins of that tequila all the way back to the exact field where the blue agaves were planted years before.

Opposite page: Tequila is bottled on a mechanized bottling line.

THE METHANOL BOGEYMAN

Methanol levels in tequila are controversial and widely misunderstood, even within the industry. Many believe that the outdated, overly strict limits on methanol levels in tequila discourage traditional agave cooking and distillation methods and reduce aroma and flavor without offering any health or safety benefits.

Methanol is a type of alcohol. Methanol itself is less toxic than the ethanol you seek out precisely for its intoxicating effects. But when your body processes methanol, it produces some truly nasty compounds that can cause serious health problems. Methanol is therefore regulated in spirits worldwide.

In tequila, methanol is a by-product of the breakdown of lignin cellulose. Lignin makes up the cell walls that help agaves retain water and maintain their physical defenses against predators. In fruit wines and brandies, methanol is a by-product of the breakdown of pectin, prevalent in apples, pears, citrus, and stone fruits.

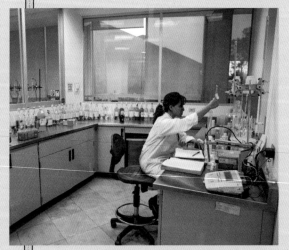

In Mexico, the limit of methanol in any beverage is 300 milligrams per 100 milliliters of pure ethanol. The United States allows twice that much for some beverages, and the European Union (known for its strict consumer protection laws) allows four times as much in certain fruit brandies. What gives?

The higher levels allowed in the United States and the European Union reflect the reality that methanol intoxication is nearly impossible with commercially produced booze. Horror stories of poisoning and even death in contemporary times result from the illegal adulteration of liquor with pure methanol. The US and EU limits for different beverage types are based on how much methanol can be produced naturally from their respective sugar sources.

By contrast, Mexico's methanol limit for all beverage types is based on wine regulations from 1986. Grapes do not contain high levels of pectin, so methanol isn't an issue for vintners. In wine, 300 milligrams is a reasonable limit, as it would have to be adulterated to get above that level. Whether or not it was ever appropriate to apply wine standards to tequila, Mexico's current regulations are simply not up-to-date with the state of research into methanol.

Scientists now know that methanol's harmful metabolites are less toxic in the presence of ethanol. When the body is busy processing ethanol, methanol passes through harmlessly. In fact, hospitals treat methanol poisoning by having the patient drink alcoholic beverages to the point of intoxication! Quite simply, you would have to drink enough of any non-adulterated beverage to poison yourself with ethanol long before you imbibed a dangerous level of methanol. Likewise, you could hypothetically poison yourself with methanol from eating dozens of apples at once. But there is no legal limit on apple consumption in any country.

Because of the agave's physical makeup, tequila (like fruit brandy) has inherently higher methanol levels than other types of spirits. The amount of methanol in traditionally produced tequila is not unsafe. However, Mexico's wine-based methanol limit encourages practices that lower methanol levels like diffuser hydrolysis, column distillation, and distilling to a high level of purity and then diluting with lots of water. These industrial methods reduce not only methanol but also the flavorful congeners found alongside it. Current methanol regulations both penalize more traditional producers and deprive tequila drinkers of aroma and flavor, without any benefit.

Opposite: A CRT lab technician analyzes the chemical content of tequila samples.

CHAPTER 3

PERSONIFYING TEQUILA

DISTILLERIES AND DISTILLERS

WHO MAKES TEQUILA?

T equila doesn't make itself. Tequila is made by people, and every tequila expresses something about those who created it, regardless of whether they worked artistically or haphazardly, or were motivated purely by profit. Tequila is not just agave, region, process, and regulation. It is the rich, tangled history of Mexican families and of Mexico itself.

Knowing the names, faces, families, and histories of the tequila industry adds to your ability to appreciate tequila. It isn't so easy to put a human face on the massive companies that produce most of the world's tequila. The giants of the industry, José Cuervo, Patrón, Sauza, and Herradura, are, after all, themselves part of the giant multinational corporations Becle SA, Bacardí, Beam Suntory, and Brown Forman, respectively. In addition to the relatively anonymous structure of such companies, the oldest of them have histories that cast long shadows and are arguably more important than who may be at the helm now. The stories of Cuervo and Sauza are inseparable from tequila itself, and both were responsible for creating a real tequila industry in the late nineteenth century. For nearly a century, Herradura was the staunch guardian of 100% agave tequila and the entrée to that category for many North Americans in the 1980s and 1990s. In many ways, that mantle was passed to Patrón in the twenty-first century. Patrón doesn't have the same historical pedigree as the others, but the company has surged to become the second-best-selling tequila in the world in a unique way that is unlikely to be replicated. Together, these four houses produce around half of all tequila in the world.

Volume isn't usually compatible with the maintenance of tradition, however. Tapatío, Siete Leguas, and Pueblo Viejo—the defenders of tradition—have all steered a path to success by staying small and remaining true to their own versions of authenticity. Tapatío and Siete Leguas are stalwarts who never gave up on producing exclusively 100% agave tequila the way it was made at the turn of the century. Both have snubbed opportunities to take on the visions of others that would compromise their own. Pueblo Viejo, a newer brand with roots in the nineteenth century, has diversified its offerings into mixtos and dabbled in more industrial methods. But under two consecutive owners, the company has earned its reputation as a progressive leader with a rich historical legacy.

For most of the history of tequila, distillers and agave growers have been at odds—sometimes even at war. The Partida, Montes, and Vivanco families are far from the first or only agaveros turned tequileros. But as founders of the Cava de Oro, Don Abraham, and Viva México brands, they are exemplary of a moment in the late twentieth century, when farmers got sick of dealing with the constant uncertainty of agave prices and threw down on their own distilleries. These families have given their children lives their grandparents could have never dreamed of by daring to go out on their own.

Generational succession is an important theme in all these stories. But Cascahuín, Don Fulano, and Arette exemplify an ascendant generation, part of a reorientation of the families' brands toward twenty-first-century niche markets that value authenticity, family history, and quality over quantity.

Some of the most exciting names in tequila might induce a sense of déjà vu. These innovators with pedigrees, Ocho, G4, Fortaleza, and Lalo are the contemporary projects of legacy tequila families, proving that everything old eventually becomes new again.

Finally, Alfredo Ríos and Javier Jiménez operate outside the system altogether and are not technically making tequila according to regulations, but both are producing highly coveted, traditional blue agave distillate within the heartland of the Tequila region. They learned their craft as the descendants of generations of tequileros and are avatars of tequila's origins. Their families represent traditions that tequila's Denomination of Origin system has arguably failed to uphold and protect.

DISTILLERIES AND BRANDS
WHAT'S THE DIFFERENCE?

Distilleries, distillers, brands, labels, marques, SKUs . . . Individual tequilas can be identified in various, often overlapping, ways that can cause confusion.

The first distinction to make is between tequila distilleries and tequila brands. A distillery is a physical place where tequila is made with CRT approval. As of 2023, there were more than 140 certified tequila distilleries. Together, they produce more than 2,600 tequila brands, or labels.

A single brand consists of one or more "marques." Commonly, a brand has three marques: a blanco, a reposado, and an añejo. But if a brand offers all five classes of tequila (adding joven and extra-añejo) in both categories (tequila and 100% agave tequila), they have ten marques. They may also have products like flavored tequilas, a cristalino, single-barrel releases, or special-edition bottles for the holidays. One brand may have well over twenty marques. In the industry, marques are also called stock-keeping units (SKUs), which are the scannable bar codes on everything you buy at the store—a more intuitive concept than "marque" for most people.

Most distilleries make a handful of brands, some make dozens, and a few make only a single brand. For example, the US whiskey company Brown Forman (NOM 1119) owns the San José del Refugio tequila distillery, commonly known as the Herradura distillery. They produce seven brands there: Herradura, Antiguo de Herradura, El Jimador, Don Eduardo, Hacienda del Cristero, Pepe López, and Suave 35. Hacienda del Cristero is made only as a 100% agave blanco, a single SKU. The Herradura brand, by contrast, has more than a dozen SKUs, all 100% agave. Not all these products are available in all countries. Some are exclusive to Mexico, some to the US. Each of these brands is owned by Brown Forman, and all are made at the same distillery.

Opposite page: More than 2,000 tequilas for sale in Tlaquepaque, Jalisco.

The distillery Casa Maestri (NOM 1438) produces more than 100 different brands in any given year. Some of these brands are owned by the distillery. But most of them are *maquilas*, or "contract brands." These are brands owned by a third party, from any country, that contracts with an authorized tequila distillery to produce a brand using that distillery owner's NOM number. Contract brands sign an agreement of co-responsibility with the producer, by which the CRT allows the brand to use the producer's NOM number on their labels.

Contract brands are often maligned by aficionados, perhaps unfairly. Such critique assumes that a tequila producer is going to make their best tequila for their own brand and won't make contract brands that are good enough to compete with the house brand. And many tequila fans prefer to support the distillery-owning families directly by buying their house brands rather than support a third party that likely has little connection to Mexico or tequila culture.

However, contract brands vary widely in character. Some have owners who are actively involved in production decisions and have

strong, ongoing partnerships with "their" tequilero. Many more come up with a brand idea and bottle design and go shopping for any producer that can fill those bottles cheaply. And that difference is not always reflected in the retail price.

At the other end of the spectrum are distilleries like Siete Leguas (NOM 1120) and El Tequileño (NOM 1108), which make a single, family-owned brand.

DISTILLERIES AND BRANDS: WHAT'S THE DIFFERENCE?

The hypothetical examples below illustrate a few of many possible relationships between distilleries, NOMs, brands, and marques or SKUs.

In the first example, Distillery 1 has a single NOM number (1234) and makes two brands. Brand A has three marques (tequila products, or SKUs), and Brand B also has three marques.

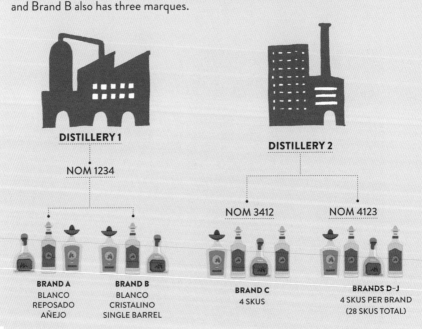

DISTILLERY 1

NOM 1234

DISTILLERY 2

NOM 3412   NOM 4123

BRAND A	BRAND B	BRAND C	BRANDS D–J
BLANCO	BLANCO	4 SKUS	4 SKUS PER BRAND
REPOSADO	CRISTALINO		(28 SKUS TOTAL)
AÑEJO	SINGLE BARREL		

Every month, the CRT releases a list of all authorized distilleries and brands. The numbers fluctuate, as distilleries shut down temporarily and new ones are built, and many contract brands are produced once, flame out in the market, and are never heard of again. The numbers of both distilleries and tequila brands have increased steadily over the past fifty years, but there are questions about how long that can continue (see Afterword, page 226).

In the second example, Distillery 2 produces tequila under two different NOMs. Under NOM 3412, it makes a single brand with four marques. And under NOM 4123, it produces seven brands (D–J), each with four marques.

In the third example, Distillery 3 and Distillery 4 are owned by the same company and share the same NOM (2341). Under this NOM, one brand, K, has three marques while six other brands (L–Q) each make four marques.

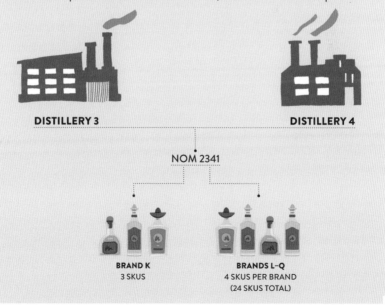

DISTILLERY 3   **DISTILLERY 4**

NOM 2341

BRAND K
3 SKUS

BRANDS L–Q
4 SKUS PER BRAND
(24 SKUS TOTAL)

BIG TEQUILA,
LITTLE TEQUILA

It seems that the tequila industry suffers from a personality crisis. On the one hand, tequila is a unique cultural product, as reflected by its status as a Geographical Indication, which limits where it can be produced. These spatial boundaries should logically impose some cap on how much tequila can be produced, yet tequila seems to be everywhere.

Dive bars, posh resorts, and every airport bar in the world offer at least one or two tequilas. This type of success is only possible because the tequila industry has welcomed multinationals like Diageo, Bacardí, Suntory, and Pernod-Ricard as owners and distributors. Now that tequila has been integrated into the global capitalist commodity system, growth must be pursued for its own sake: growth in production, exports, sales, and market share.

This tension between an exclusivity rooted in a specific place and the market imperative for limitless growth is the defining feature of tequila in the twenty-first century. The result is that the tequila industry is bifurcated into an industrial segment and an artisanal segment. We can expect the division between these two branches to widen in coming years.

Tequila's bicephalous nature means it's impossible to talk about what "most tequila" is like without first defining terms. By volume, a handful of companies—José Cuervo, Patrón, Sauza, Don Julio, and Herradura—accounted for more than half of all tequila sales in the world in 2020. Adding the next nine producers—for a total of only fourteen—takes you up to 75% of global sales. In terms of corporate ownership, three companies accounted for half of global market share in 2020, with about 70% claimed by eight companies. This ocean of tequila is made in large volumes for the world market and is pushed by expensive and sophisticated marketing campaigns. *This* is the tequila that most people know, and that many aficionados love to hate.

The picture is different if you're talking about "most tequila makers."

Approximately 140 producers sell the remaining 25% of all tequila. These medium, small, and micro-producers are often family owned. Their volume depends more on agave price than consumer demand, and most are producing tequila in an arguably artisanal fashion.

At the furthest extreme are the most traditional, which make relatively tiny volumes of tequila. These tequileros depend on direct contact with consumers and bartenders to get the word out, trusting that quality will speak for itself. Crucially, they are mostly legacy tequila producers, hailing from decades- or centuries-long lineages of tequila makers. With little or no marketing budget, they rely on storytelling and hand-selling. Most have diversified wealth and can afford to lose money on tequila in years when agave prices are high. This is the unfair reality: Making a living from tequila is a prerogative of the rich, and it always has been.

No one is going to break into the elite inner circle that dominates global market share. The behemoths may very well continue to consolidate among themselves, however. While they will innovate in branding and marketing, their flavor profiles are likely to become even more similar as ever-advancing industrial production methods make uniformity easier to achieve.

In the crowded sector of small producers, competition is fierce. Brands and distilleries fail and change hands frequently, and this will continue. The success of brands like Fortaleza and El Tesoro de Don Felipe will persuade others to turn toward more traditional production. Historical legacies will be emphasized or invented.

The vast differences between "big tequila" and "little tequila" can make it seem like two different beverages. But tequila's two-headed nature doesn't have to be an existential threat. Consider wine. In the United States, you can buy a four-liter jug of domestic plonk for a few dollars. Or you could drop a thousand dollars on a collectible Bordeaux. Both are wines, each has its market, and neither one harms the other. In the vast middle of the price range are hundreds of brands claiming historical legacies and artisanal production—some real, some dubious. Wine persists and thrives as a category. If tequila survives the other challenges to its existence (see page 226), its split down the middle shouldn't be a problem.

JOSÉ CUERVO

The largest, the oldest, and synonymous with tequila throughout the world.

NOM: 1122

BRAND ESTABLISHED: 1934

DISTILLERIES:
La Rojeña (est. 1796) & Los Camichines

OTHER BRANDS INCLUDE:
Tradicional, Maestro Dobel, 1800, Reserva de la Familia, Gran Centenario

AGAVE SOURCE:
DOT-wide

HYDROLYSIS:
Diffuser, stone oven

EXTRACTION:
Diffuser, roller mill

FERMENTATION:
Sealed stainless-steel vats

DISTILLATION:
Column, copper pot

BARRELS:
Used American oak

José Cuervo is the largest tequila company in the world and is likely to remain so well into the future. Cuervo produces 20% of all tequila—more than its two closest rivals, Patrón and Sauza, combined. Despite going public in 2017, Cuervo remains fairly opaque about specifics of its tequila production. The historic part of their La Rojeña distillery in the center of Tequila town is open to the public, but the massive, industrial Los Camichines factory east of Guadalajara is not. It is anyone's guess which of their tequilas are made where, although most of their 100 million liters a year are likely made outside of La Rojeña.

Outside of North America, José Cuervo is often the only tequila people know: Cuervo *is* the tequila category. In the United States, the brand is frequently maligned by those who overdid it with Cuervo Gold shots and syrupy margaritas in their youth. In fact, Casa Cuervo produces a gamut of tequilas, ranging from the cheapest mixto gold to exclusive extra-añejos that garner hundreds of dollars a bottle. Their Reserva de la Familia añejo is released in collectible wooden boxes designed by different Mexican artists each year. Reserva continues to be an entry point for many an aficionado into the world of 100% agave tequila.

In addition to being the biggest, Cuervo also claims the

longest lineage in the tequila industry. In 1795, José Cuervo y Montaño became the first tequilero to receive permission from the Spanish Crown to produce tequila for sale, something he had already been doing for more than forty years.

By the late nineteenth century, the La Rojeña distillery had passed into the hands of Jesús Flores. Flores was in fierce competition with Cenobio Sauza to modernize tequila production and expand sales outside of the region. Among his many innovations, in 1880, Flores was the first to sell tequila in glass bottles. When he passed away in 1898, Flores left a widow, Ana González Rubio. Ana was intelligent, capable, and ambitious, but the laws and social mores of the time kept her from operating such an important company on her own, so she offered a marriage of convenience and mutual benefit to José Cuervo Labastida, who was already a trusted administrator of La Rojeña.

Ana and José made out like bandits during the Mexican Revolution, acquiring land and valuable properties in Guadalajara and Mexico City while many of their contemporaries were driven into exile or fell into ruin. It was in this era that they started selling tequila under the "José Cuervo" label. Their marriage produced no offspring, and although fifteen years his senior, Ana González survived José Cuervo. Ultimately, she bequeathed the business to her niece, Guadalupe Gallardo. Gallardo in turn left the company to her nephew, Juan Francisco Beckmann Gallardo.

Beckmann took over the company in 1966. His son, Juan Beckmann Vidal, presided over Cuervo's $900 million IPO in 2017. Beckmann and his children remain the largest shareholders and are regularly listed as among the ten richest families in Mexico.

PATRÓN

An anomalous brand that changed the industry forever
by producing industrial volumes of artisanal tequila.

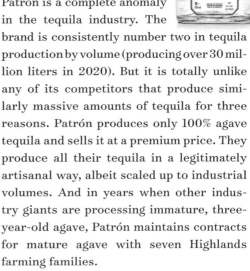

NOM: 1492

BRAND ESTABLISHED:
1989

DISTILLERY:
Hacienda Patrón (Atotonilco
El Alto, Jalisco, est. 2009)

OTHER BRANDS INCLUDE:
Roca Patrón

AGAVE SOURCE:
Highlands

HYDROLYSIS:
Stone oven

EXTRACTION:
Roller mill, tahona

FERMENTATION:
Open wood vats
(some with fiber)

DISTILLATION:
Copper pot (some with fiber)

BARRELS:
Used American oak, French
and Hungarian oak

Patrón is a complete anomaly in the tequila industry. The brand is consistently number two in tequila production by volume (producing over 30 million liters in 2020). But it is totally unlike any of its competitors that produce similarly massive amounts of tequila for three reasons. Patrón produces only 100% agave tequila and sells it at a premium price. They produce all their tequila in a legitimately artisanal way, albeit scaled up to industrial volumes. And in years when other industry giants are processing immature, three-year-old agave, Patrón maintains contracts for mature agave with seven Highlands farming families.

In 1989, Patrón began life as the only contract brand ever produced by Siete Leguas (page 146). That relationship ended acrimoniously when the late Francisco Alcaraz left Siete Leguas with Patrón in 2002. In a new distillery, Alcaraz replicated and magnified the Siete Leguas process that he had helped develop. Patrón owner Juan Paul Dejoria always knew he wanted Patrón to be a giant of the tequila industry, and the new distillery was built with massive expansion in mind.

There is something discordant about entering the Patrón factory and seeing more than fifteen motorized tahonas, long rows of wooden fermentation vats capped with agave fiber, and dozens of pure-copper alembic stills. These are centuries-old techniques, generally found in distilleries a fraction of the size that do less than 10% of the volume of Patrón. The tequila produced in this scaled-up traditional production line is blended with tequila produced in the same distillery on a

more efficient line, with roller-mill extraction, fermentation without fiber in stainless-steel tanks, and alembic distillation of liquid-only fermented mosto. Patrón had the confidence and foresight to build a modular distillery with a huge footprint, which has allowed it to add tahonas, vats, and stills over the years. In this way it became the first brand capable of mass-producing artisanal tequila.

Much of Patrón's success had to do with timing: Good tequila in nice bottles marketed as a status symbol was right on time in the 1990s. Patrón's early success as a slick nightclub tequila, followed by its ubiquity on grocery store shelves, has long made it a frequent target for demonization by tequila aficionados and liquor purists—many of whom consider Patrón to be the devil incarnate. To hundreds of thousands of US consumers, however, Patrón was the best tequila they had ever tasted. In the early 1990s, the market was awash in mixtos, and Patrón's huge distribution network made it the first 100% agave tequila that many Americans had ever tried. Patrón is filtered to give it a "smoothness" that appeals to tequila novices and shot-takers, but it has always been a well-made tequila.

In 2018, global liquor giant Bacardí purchased Patrón for more than $5 billion. Tequila aficionados are watching closely to see if the new owners can continue to pull off the neat trick of making the world's only mass-produced artisanal tequila.

SAUZA

A storied tequila company whose tradition is
inseparable from technological innovation.

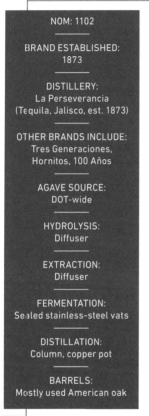

NOM: 1102

BRAND ESTABLISHED:
1873

DISTILLERY:
La Perseverancia
(Tequila, Jalisco, est. 1873)

OTHER BRANDS INCLUDE:
Tres Generaciones,
Hornitos, 100 Años

AGAVE SOURCE:
DOT-wide

HYDROLYSIS:
Diffuser

EXTRACTION:
Diffuser

FERMENTATION:
Sealed stainless-steel vats

DISTILLATION:
Column, copper pot

BARRELS:
Mostly used American oak

Sauza is the second- or third-largest producer of tequila in any given year. Its only distillery, La Perseverancia, in Tequila, uses cutting-edge technology to produce nearly 30 million liters annually. Among industrial producers using the diffuser method (see page 87), Sauza is the only company that not only is transparent about its process but proudly centers it as part of their identity. This open embrace of the latest technology is consistent with the brand's historic legacy, as Sauza has been at the vanguard of industrial innovation since the beginning.

The Sauza story begins in 1858, when a sixteen-year-old Cenobio Sauza came to Tequila to work as an administrator for José Antonio Gómez Cuervo. Ambitious, intelligent, and ruthless, Cenobio quickly learned the tequila business and wasted no time in building his own empire, which would come to dominate the industry through much of the twentieth century. The Sauza and Cuervo dynasties would develop a legendary rivalry that continues to this day.

Cenobio acquired his first distillery in 1873, which he renamed La Perseverancia. That same year, he famously sent thirteen barrels and six glass damajuanas of vino mezcal to El Paso by mule train. Although others had already exported tequila to the United

States by then, they remain obscure historical footnotes. Sauza has paperwork documenting the 1873 shipment and has used it to lay claim to the first legal tequila export.

By the end of the century, Cenobio Sauza was one of the largest landowners and distillers in Jalisco and was racking up gold medals in spirits competitions throughout the United States. He was among the first tequileros to introduce steam-cooking and continuous distillation in columns. He was also responsible for the first blue agave being planted in the Jalisco Highlands, in response to an agave blight in the 1870s.

Cenobio's son Eladio oversaw the transition into the twentieth century and throughout the turbulent periods of the Mexican Revolution, US Prohibition, and World War II. In turn, Eladio's son, Francisco Javier, brought tequila (and Sauza) to the rest of the world through expansion, further modernization of production, helping to create the Denomination of Origin for Tequila, and ultimately making the tequila industry's first sale to a large liquor conglomerate.

Cenobio, Eladio, and Francisco Javier are known as the *Tres Generaciones* (three generations) of Sauza's premium brand. Francisco Javier had a gift for marketing and placed the likenesses of himself, his father, and his grandfather on the label. At a time when perennial rival Cuervo had stripped almost all history from

its image abroad, Francisco Javier recognized the value in his family's unique and historic contributions to tequila.

Sauza was the world's leading tequila brand and one of the most technologically advanced when Francisco Javier sold it to the Spanish brandy company Pedro Domecq in 1976. The company went through a series of sales as it ceded its market dominance to Cuervo in the 1980s and 1990s. Today, Sauza is owned by the Japanese whiskey giant Beam Suntory.

HERRADURA

The most famous tequila from Amatitán, the spirit's likely birthplace.

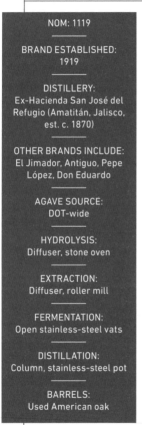

NOM: 1119

BRAND ESTABLISHED:
1919

DISTILLERY:
Ex-Hacienda San José del
Refugio (Amatitán, Jalisco,
est. c. 1870)

OTHER BRANDS INCLUDE:
El Jimador, Antiguo, Pepe
López, Don Eduardo

AGAVE SOURCE:
DOT-wide

HYDROLYSIS:
Diffuser, stone oven

EXTRACTION:
Diffuser, roller mill

FERMENTATION:
Open stainless-steel vats

DISTILLATION:
Column, stainless-steel pot

BARRELS:
Used American oak

Herradura was the first 100% agave tequila brand regularly and legally imported to the United States. American crooner Bing Crosby became so enamored with Herradura on his frequent jaunts to Acapulco that in 1955 he started an import company to share it with his show business pals. For the next twenty-five years, if you had 100% agave in the United States, it almost certainly had a horseshoe (*una herradura*) on the label.

Herradura tequilas are made at the Ex-Hacienda San José del Refugio in Amatitán, not far from tequila's likely birthplace (see page 14). The hacienda and its distillery belonged to a priest named Feliciano Romo, who bequeathed his property to Josefina Salazar and her sister in 1861. A local named Félix López ran the distillery and produced tequila for the sisters, reportedly without pay. He was rewarded mightily when the childless Josefina Salazar passed away and left him the hacienda in 1874.

López and his wife, Carmen Rosales (who came from a tequila family in nearby El Arenal), shepherded the hacienda through the Mexican Revolution, when they even managed to expand and consolidate land around San José del Refugio. Their son, Aurelio, inherited the hacienda and ran it with his cousin, David Rosales.

Aurelio, David, and other relatives including Alfonso Jiménez (see Caballito Cerrero, page 174) started the Herradura brand in 1919, although it wasn't registered legally until 1928. Aurelio was a devout Catholic even by local standards, and when the Cristero civil war broke out between the federal government and Church supporters in 1926, he was heavily involved in the armed uprising. Federal troops shut down the distillery for a time, and Aurelio was exiled to the Vatican in 1927.

Upon Aurelio's death, he left everything to David, who was also childless. Upon his death, David left the company to his sister, whose daughter married Guillermo Romo de la Peña, thus bringing the Romo name back into ownership of the hacienda and distillery.

The Romo family brought Herradura into the modern era and international markets without changing the artisanal nature of the tequila. The original distillery, with its tahona and in-ground stone fermentation vats, wasn't retired until 1963. The Romos did tequila lovers a great service by preserving that structure while most of their contemporaries were demolishing similar ones. Contemporary visitors to Herradura can walk through the original distillery. It is one of the most evocative experiences in the tequila world.

Guillermo Romo was the leader and protector of a small group of traditional producers who refused to make anything less than 100% agave tequila. The group successfully fought to change US import policies so that 100% agave tequila was no longer taxed at a higher rate than mixto.

Herradura wasn't opposed to innovation, though. The company successfully lobbied for creation of the reposado (1974) and extra-añejo (2005) classes of tequila.

The Romos sold Herradura to Brown Forman, the makers of Jack Daniels, in 2007.

TAPATÍO

Highlands pioneers who kept tequila traditions alive through lean and trying times.

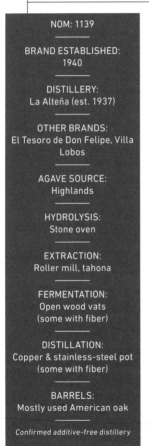

NOM: 1139

BRAND ESTABLISHED:
1940

DISTILLERY:
La Alteña (est. 1937)

OTHER BRANDS:
El Tesoro de Don Felipe, Villa Lobos

AGAVE SOURCE:
Highlands

HYDROLYSIS:
Stone oven

EXTRACTION:
Roller mill, tahona

FERMENTATION:
Open wood vats
(some with fiber)

DISTILLATION:
Copper & stainless-steel pot
(some with fiber)

BARRELS:
Mostly used American oak

Confirmed additive-free distillery

Tapatío's distillery, La Alteña, is one of the most renowned in the tequila industry. There, the Camarena family has made some of the most consistently delicious tequilas ever and has maintained traditional production methods all the while.

The Camarenas were tequila pioneers in the Highlands. Pedro Camarena Ramírez began farming blue agave and built a distillery near Arandas in the 1880s. During both the Mexican Revolution (1910–1921) and the Cristero War (1926–1929), the family was forced to abandon the original adobe distillery, and it eventually fell into ruin. At the end of the conflicts, the family returned from Arandas to the countryside, resumed farming agave, and built a new distillery—La Alteña—in 1937. Being both agave farmers and tequila distillers has always been key to the family's success, as it allows them to maintain high standards of quality in raw material and insulates them to some degree from fluctuations in agave price.

Pedro's son, Don Felipe Camarena Sr., took over production at La Alteña and began producing the tequila that would come to be named Tequila Tapatío. It garnered a solidly loyal customer base in Arandas, and its reputation grew. In 1988, the American entrepreneurs Bob Denton and Marilyn Smith came calling. Denton and Smith were looking for an excellent 100% agave tequila to import after they had problems with Chinaco in Tamaulipas. Together, the trio of Felipe Sr., Denton, and Smith created the brand El Tesoro de Don Felipe, the first export tequila from La Alteña. Denton and Smith lovingly hand-sold El Tesoro throughout the United States, teaching thousands of Americans what quality 100% agave tequila tasted like. Without El Tesoro, there may not have been a tequila boom in the 1990s.

Don Felipe passed away in 2003. The La Alteña distillery and the Tapatío brand are now owned by his children and their families. Sons Felipe Jr. and Carlos have built their own distilleries (see G4, page 166, and Ocho, page 164). La Alteña's flagship brands remain Tapatío and El Tesoro de Don Felipe (owned by Beam Suntory). Daughters Jennifer, Gabriela, and Liliana now run the distillery.

The family has augmented La Alteña's historic production line with slightly more modern touches to create distinct flavor profiles for different brands. All Alteña tequilas begin with mature, oven-cooked agave. El Tesoro is tahona-milled, the aguamiel is fermented with fiber, and the mosto is double-distilled in 350-liter copper alembics. Tapatío is produced in a hybrid process, combining the El Tesoro methods with roller mill extraction, fermentation without fiber, first distillation in stainless steel, and second distillation in copper. With their bold, agave-forward flavors, both tequilas continue to blow the minds of tequila newcomers while remaining stalwart favorites of veteran aficionados.

SIETE LEGUAS

A quintessential tequila drinker's tequila, and the last to be made with mule-drawn tahonas.

NOM: 1120

BRAND ESTABLISHED:
1952

DISTILLERIES:
El Centenario (1952), La
Vencedora (1981) & La
Victoria (2022)

OTHER BRANDS:
none

AGAVE SOURCE:
Highlands

HYDROLYSIS:
Stone oven

EXTRACTION:
Roller mill & tahona

FERMENTATION:
Open stainless-steel vats
(some with fiber)

DISTILLATION:
Copper pot (some with fiber)

BARRELS:
Used American oak

Confirmed additive-free distillery

Siete Leguas may be the most important tequila that most Americans have never heard of. It is also among a tiny handful of Mexican family-owned distilleries making a single brand exclusively.

Don Ignacio González Vargas learned to make tequila as a young man working in Atotonilco el Alto alongside his cousin Julio. In 1952, Ignacio bought the Centenario distillery and founded Tequila Siete Leguas. Siete Leguas was the name of Mexican revolutionary Pancho Villa's favorite horse, which inspired a popular folk song of the same name. "Seven leagues," the English translation, is how far a horse could ride in a single day through the countryside—about twenty-one miles.

Over time, Siete Leguas became the preferred tequila in Atotonilco and was also quite popular in Guadalajara. The González family was in extremely rare company, producing only 100% agave tequila, never deigning to make mixto even during the agave crisis of the 1980s.

In 1981, the company expanded its production to include a second distillery, La Vencedora, which is right up the street from the first. This expansion allowed them to increase production by introducing roller mills and larger fermentation tanks and stills. Since then, Siete Leguas blanco has been a proprietary blend of the tequilas produced at La Vencedora and El Centenario. El Centenario's process may be considered the most traditional in tequila, as fermentation and distillation are both with agave fiber, and the tahona extraction is still powered by mules, which is unique in the industry. In 2022, they expanded again, adding the La Victoria distillery, which also features tahona and agave fiber production. The proportion of each distillery's tequila in bottled Siete Leguas blanco is a closely guarded secret, and it is the product of meticulous blending by an in-house tasting panel, so the precise blend may change from batch to batch.

The resulting blanco is unmistakably unique: peppery and dry with a strong backbone of cooked agave. The other expressions are lightly aged, producing a line of tequilas in which the agave is present all the way into the extra-añejo, called D'Antaño.

Today, Siete Leguas is run by Don Ignacio's son, Fernando González de Anda. Fernando is a magnanimous family man who doesn't like to be too far from Atotonilco and the distillery— in fact, he lives right up the street. He also isn't particularly interested in marketing or playing the game in the United States. Rather than spend money on advertising, sales incentives, and promotional swag, he prefers to let the tequila speak for itself. Because of Siete Leguas's longstanding import relationship with Sazerac, it is available in most US states, albeit not heavily promoted.

Fernando shies away from discussion of other brands, focusing intensely on his own tequila. But his family tree is also remarkable. Don Ignacio's cousin Julio would later be known as "Don" Julio, and he produced a successful tequila of his own across town. And Patrón (page 138) owes its early success to originally being Siete Leguas in a different bottle; that was the only contract brand the family has ever made. For Fernando, these brief associations with global giants are nothing to brag about—his pride is centered on remaining true to his family's traditions as he steadfastly guides Siete Leguas into the future.

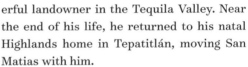

PUEBLO VIEJO

Home of one of the industry's oldest lineages, where the tequila is produced and owned by visionary women.

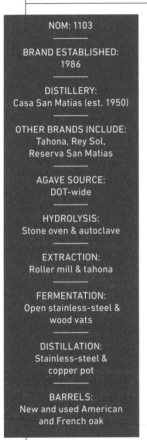

NOM: 1103

BRAND ESTABLISHED:
1986

DISTILLERY:
Casa San Matias (est. 1950)

OTHER BRANDS INCLUDE:
Tahona, Rey Sol,
Reserva San Matias

AGAVE SOURCE:
DOT-wide

HYDROLYSIS:
Stone oven & autoclave

EXTRACTION:
Roller mill & tahona

FERMENTATION:
Open stainless-steel &
wood vats

DISTILLATION:
Stainless-steel &
copper pot

BARRELS:
New and used American
and French oak

Casa San Matias has done an incredible job successfully transitioning through historical epochs. It is one of the oldest existing tequila companies, having started in Magadalena around 1886 before moving to Tequila in 1912. San Matias was founded by Delfino González, a powerful landowner in the Tequila Valley. Near the end of his life, he returned to his natal Highlands home in Tepatitlán, moving San Matias with him.

In 1986, Jesús Román bought San Matias with plans to return production to 100% agave tequila. In just over a decade, Román made a massive mark on the tequila industry. He launched the Pueblo Viejo brand, and it is still the flagship of Casa San Matias. He was a particularly outspoken critic of the unfair advantages afforded to the mixto category of tequila (see Two Categories of Tequila, page 50), advocating for the mandatory bottling of all tequila within the DOT and joining other tequileros in having the US import taxes on 100% agave tequila lowered to be on par with those on tequila mixto and other liquors in the early 1990s.

After Román's untimely death in 1997, his widow, Carmen Villareal, took over the company, and she runs it to this day.

Villareal's intelligent and humane leadership has guided San Matias out of tragedy and into a twenty-first-century rebirth. In 1998, she commissioned legendary Guadalajara artist Sergio Bustamante to design the bottle for Rey Sol—an exquisite French oak extra-añejo in one of the most collectible packages ever.

Pueblo Viejo's high quality-to-price ratio made it a go-to tequila for Jaliscan immigrants to the United States well before it was on the radar of cocktail bartenders. But those bartenders made up for lost time in the late 2010s, when it became common to see Pueblo Viejo as the well tequila in the country's best cocktail bars. San Matias released a 104-proof version of Pueblo Viejo blanco in 2015, specifically for use in cocktails. In 2016, San Matias joined the movement of tequilas returning to traditional methods, installing a tahona to produce a new brand called Tahona.

Villareal is recognized throughout Mexico for her commitment to women's rights and progressive causes. She was the first woman CEO of a tequila company and to this day is the only one who owns and operates her own distillery. Since 2007, all San Matias tequilas have been produced by *maestra tequilera* Rocío Rodriguez, a brilliant chemist and one of the few women in charge of tequila production.

With a mix of humility and wit, Villareal tends to downplay her role as a trailblazer. To the constant question "What is it like to be a female tequila maker," she replies with a winning smile: "Why don't you ask the men what it is like for them?"

CELEBRITY TEQUILAS

These days, it seems like every week another celebrity begins hawking their own tequila. From basketball legends Michael Jordan and LeBron James, to country musicians like George Strait, pop stars Adam Levine and Nick Jonas, and actors Kevin Hart and Eva Longoria, the rich and famous have proliferated as owners, investors, and ambassadors for dozens of tequila brands.

While these deals have multiplied since the early 2000s, celebrity tequilas are older than you might think. Legendary crooner Bing Crosby became the first US importer of 100% agave tequila when he introduced Herradura to the country in 1955. In 1999, rocker Sammy Hagar launched Cabo Wabo in the United States, selling it to Campari for more than $90 million in 2010. Cabo Wabo was an early entry point to tequila for many people who would become serious tequila aficionados and collectors.

Although Hagar's payout seemed colossal at the time, it was dwarfed in 2017. That year, Hollywood heartthrob George Clooney and his partners sold their Casamigos brand to Diageo for $1 billion only four years after it launched. Like the Cabo Wabo deal, this sale was just for a brand: neither a distillery nor a single agave plant was sold. Again, this latest deal seemed like it could never be topped. But three years later, actor and former pro wrestler Dwayne "The Rock" Johnson launched the brand Teremana in 2020. It reportedly sold nearly 400,000 cases in its first year, and some insiders predict it will ultimately sell for as much as $2 billion. In 2022, Casamigos was one of the ten top-selling tequilas in the world, and Teremana was not far behind it in US sales.

Casamigos and Teremana indicate the upsides of celebrity brands for both their founders and the corporations that distribute and eventually buy them. The stars are making an investment in a rapidly growing category that involves little work on their part. Giant spirits companies get a brand with invaluable ready-made marketing, allowing them to leapfrog over the otherwise arduous process of building one from scratch.

What's not to like, right? For tequila purists, quite a lot, actually. Many resent that the attention focused on (usually non-Mexican) celebrities obscures the fact that tequila is made in Jalisco with Mexican labor and know-how. Model and socialite Kendall Jenner faced accusations of cultural appropriation upon launching her tequila brand, 818, in 2021. Some decried this as a sexist double standard because high-profile men like Justin Timberlake were getting a pass as tequila brand owners.

A more widespread criticism of celebrity tequilas is that they masquerade as unique products developed for (or even by) their star owners when that is never the case. While most famous tequila pitchmen tell similar stories of "falling in love" with tequila, "knocking on doors" of distilleries, visiting Jalisco countless times, and ultimately developing "their own" perfect tequila recipe, in reality, all of these tequilas are contract brands. A small number of distilleries produce them, and most of the tequila is made exactly as it is for that distillery's other brands, with a different blend of additives as the most frequent distinction. But the star's name justifies a higher price point, and consumers are really paying to feel an association with someone they admire.

Nevertheless, some craft tequila makers welcome celebrity tequilas as a type of free publicity for the entire category, and they certainly have a point. Going all the way back to Bing and Sammy, some people who are drawn to tequila by the glimmer of fame will eventually graduate to better, more authentic tequilas.

CAVA DE ORO

A multi-generational agave-growing family with a Cinderella story of sweet, crowd-pleasing tequila that snobs love to hate.

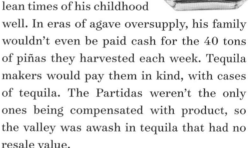

NOM: 1477

BRAND ESTABLISHED:
1999

DISTILLERY:
Cava de Oro (est. 1999)

OTHER BRANDS INCLUDE:
Adictivo, Gran Reserva de
Don Alberto, Amatiteña

AGAVE SOURCE:
Tequila Valley

HYDROLYSIS:
Stone oven

EXTRACTION:
Roller mill

FERMENTATION:
Open stainless-steel vats

DISTILLATION:
Stainless-steel pot

BARRELS:
Used French oak

Amatiteña is a confirmed additive-free brand

Alberto Partida Hermosillo is a young man, born in 1988. But the Cava de Oro co-owner remembers the lean times of his childhood well. In eras of agave oversupply, his family wouldn't even be paid cash for the 40 tons of piñas they harvested each week. Tequila makers would pay them in kind, with cases of tequila. The Partidas weren't the only ones being compensated with product, so the valley was awash in tequila that had no resale value.

In 1999, Alberto's parents, Gildardo and Leticia, said *ya, basta,* enough is enough, and built a distillery alongside the highway, with one brick oven and two alembic stills. The first decade was a struggle to learn to make and sell tequila. Established tequileros didn't want more competition and refused to teach them how to turn their agave into legally saleable tequila. The challenges of entering the global marketplace were even greater. For the first few years, the Partidas's tequila wasn't very good and sales were meager.

In 2010, the CRT started offering courses in production, quality control, and business practices. Alberto credits the CRT with giving his family the boost they needed to become viable tequileros. Their first brand, Cava de Oro, is still their flagship. They sell 80% of their volume in the United States, and the rest in a handful of other countries and Mexico's top tourist destinations: Los Cabos, the Riviera Maya, and Puerto Vallarta. The short, distinctive bottle is also ubiquitous in liquor stores and gift shops in the Tequila Valley.

A sip of Cava de Oro typically elicits gasps of delight from casual tourists and dismayed grimaces from many aficionados. It is one of the sweetest tequilas you will ever encounter, and exemplary of just how much the 1% volume of allowed additives can alter the profile of a tequila. Cava de Oro certainly bumps right up against the legal limit for all allowed additives, including caramel, glycerin, agave syrup, and flavoring agents.

Alberto explains that it's a flavor profile that the family enjoys, and it was enthusiastically received when they began attending trade shows and tequila expos in the United States. The success of Cava de Oro has allowed the family to branch out and offer other flavor profiles as well. While some of their brands match Cava's saccharine profile, their Amatiteña brand is confirmed additive-free and has earned praise from the same aficionados who had spared no energy in tearing down Cava de Oro over the years.

Regardless of one's take on tequilas like Cava de Oro, the Partidas's underdog success story is undeniably moving. Asked about the intense criticism of his tequila over the years, Alberto responds candidly: "At first, you take those criticisms personally, and yes, it hurts. But eventually, you learn to let it go, and recognize that everyone has their own opinion."

DON ABRAHAM

Agave farming brothers who made good—
real good—with a little help from a friend.

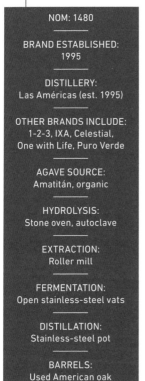

NOM: 1480

BRAND ESTABLISHED:
1995

DISTILLERY:
Las Américas (est. 1995)

OTHER BRANDS INCLUDE:
1-2-3, IXA, Celestial,
One with Life, Puro Verde

AGAVE SOURCE:
Amatitán, organic

HYDROLYSIS:
Stone oven, autoclave

EXTRACTION:
Roller mill

FERMENTATION:
Open stainless-steel vats

DISTILLATION:
Stainless-steel pot

BARRELS:
Used American oak

Abraham Montes began farming agave in Amatitán around 1920, and his grandsons Álvaro, Eladio, and Carlos were born into the family business. Historically, the family sold most of their agave to Herradura, and rode out the tumultuous agave price cycle as best they could. But, in 1997, a Highlands ice storm and subsequent crop infestation resulted in an industry-wide agave shortage and price spike. The Montes were well positioned to meet that demand with plenty of mature Valley agave that year and in subsequent years, making a windfall selling at around 15 pesos a kilogram.

Selling top-notch agave at late-1990s prices was a financial game changer for the Montes family. The brothers decided they liked having a steady income and weren't looking forward to the inevitable crash in agave price (which, in fact, happened in 2008). So in 1995, they invested in the construction of their own tequila distillery right off the highway in Amatitán.

In the 1930s, the brothers' father had worked at Herradura as a *batidor*, a physically demanding job that required immersing oneself in the fermentation vats to physically separate aguamiel from agave fiber at the beginning of the fermentation process. By the 1990s, this practice was no longer used in making tequila, but that was about all the brothers knew about tequila production, so they called Guillermo Romo and asked for help. Romo was one of the owners of Herradura at the time, and he regularly bought most of the Montes's agave crop. He was eager to help and sent a stonemason who built them an exact replica of the brick ovens at the Herradura distillery. That single brick oven at the Las Américas distillery is still where production of all the 100% agave tequila begins.

Eladio says it took a few years of mistakes before they produced anything they thought tasted good. The learning curve may have been steep, but once the Montes brothers found their formula, there was no stopping them, and things really started to take off around 2004. They initially produced a single house brand—Don Abraham, named for their grandfather. But as they slowly built a reputation for quality tequila at fair prices, contract brands from all over the world came calling. Today, the Las Américas distillery produces dozens of tequilas that are exported all over the world. In fact, some years they don't produce Don Abraham at all, as high liquor taxes in Mexico and free trade agreements make exporting other brands far more profitable.

While Las Américas tequilas have made the Montes family successful, Álvaro insists that it is all based on the quality of the agave they grow. He oversees the family's field operations, which are certified organic. Using liberal application of compost and manure and pheromone-baited insect traps, the Montes brothers grow some of the largest, sweetest, healthiest agave in the Tequila Valley. In Álvaro's words, "If I grow the best agave, how could I not make the best tequila?"

VIVA MÉXICO

The Highlands agave-farming family who have built a reputation for consistent quality while making a variety of tequilas.

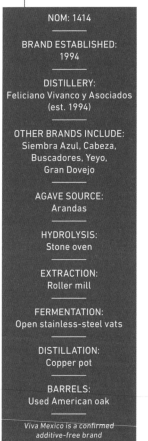

NOM: 1414

BRAND ESTABLISHED:
1994

DISTILLERY:
Feliciano Vivanco y Asociados
(est. 1994)

OTHER BRANDS INCLUDE:
Siembra Azul, Cabeza,
Buscadores, Yeyo,
Gran Dovejo

AGAVE SOURCE:
Arandas

HYDROLYSIS:
Stone oven

EXTRACTION:
Roller mill

FERMENTATION:
Open stainless-steel vats

DISTILLATION:
Copper pot

BARRELS:
Used American oak

Viva Mexico is a confirmed additive-free brand

Tequila Viva México is relatively unknown outside of Arandas. Its owners, the five Vivanco brothers, are better known for the consistently high-quality contract brands they have produced since the late 1990s. In aficionado circles, referring to the Vivancos's NOM number—a "1414 tequila"—is typically shorthand for a tequila whose quality far exceeds its price. Those in the know are likely to buy any "1414" tequila even if they haven't tried that particular brand before.

Brothers Sergio, César, Leopoldo, José Manuel, and Feliciano Jr. are fourth-generation agave farmers. Their great-uncle José was a martyr in the bloody Cristero War, publicly executed in 1929. José's grand-nephew, Feliciano Vivanco, was a hardworking agave farmer with an elementary school education. He sacrificed to make sure all five of his children received a better education, and they all went into the family business with him. The economic chaos wrought by fluctuating agave prices drove them to become tequileros as well.

From the beginning, the Vivancos knew that trying to make tequila cheaper than the industry giants was impossible, so they vowed to make only *tequilas finos*—quality tequilas that would cost a bit more but garner a loyal clientele. They figured making tequila would be easy. It wasn't. According to Sergio Vivanco, their first batch of tequila "tasted like bread" because they had fermented with a readily available bread yeast. His brother César eventually got a masters degree in tequila making, and today he oversees production at the distillery.

Feliciano Jr. manages the family's sixteen small agave ranches. This field operation provides all the agave for Viva México and their contract brands, and in many years has allowed them to sell surplus agave on the open market. This relative autonomy means that the Vivancos can be selective about taking on contract brand clients. The family takes tequila quite seriously as a source of national pride, and they don't want to make brands or work with people who could give tequila, and Mexico, a bad name.

This commitment to quality, their own mature agave, and the well water at the distillery are fundamental components of the "1414" recipe. More controversially, the Vivancos are also the best-known advocates of the so-called Mozart method: They play classical music during fermentation because the vibrations are said to facilitate more harmonious fermentation. Sergio says they actually achieve better results with Vivaldi.

Despite the old-school branding of Viva México, the Vivancos don't pine for the old days. Sergio insists that it's never been easier for the average consumer to find good tequila than it is today. And he isn't shy about listing other families in the industry who

are making excellent tequila. The point, he says, is to earn your place among those tequilas finos.

"People who drink good tequila don't get married to one brand," he says, "they get married to quality."

Feliciano Vivanco Sr., affectionately known as Don Chano, walked to work at the distillery every day until his passing at ninety-four years of age in 2016.

CASCAHUÍN

A family brand that quietly chugged along for fifty years until becoming a star in the twenty-first century.

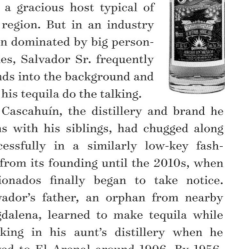

NOM: 1123

BRAND ESTABLISHED:
1956

DISTILLERY:
Cascahuín (est. 1956)

OTHER BRANDS INCLUDE:
Siembra Valles, Revolución,
Wild Common, Cuernito

AGAVE SOURCE:
El Arenal

HYDROLYSIS:
Stone oven, earthen pit

EXTRACTION:
Roller mill, tahona, mallet

FERMENTATION:
Open wood, stainless-steel
& concrete vats

DISTILLATION:
Stainless-steel &
copper pot

BARRELS:
Used American oak,
French oak

Cascahuín, Siembra Valles, and
Wild Common are confirmed
additive-free brands

Salvador Rosales Sr. is a quiet man. He is friendly, even warm, and a gracious host typical of the region. But in an industry often dominated by big personalities, Salvador Sr. frequently blends into the background and lets his tequila do the talking.

Cascahuín, the distillery and brand he owns with his siblings, had chugged along successfully in a similarly low-key fashion from its founding until the 2010s, when aficionados finally began to take notice. Salvador's father, an orphan from nearby Magdalena, learned to make tequila while working in his aunt's distillery when he moved to El Arenal around 1906. By 1956, he had built his own distillery and named his brand Casachuín, "hill of light" in the local language, referring to a nearby peak.

Business began to take off in the 1970s and 1980s as Salvador Sr. and his siblings took over and slowly got their tequila into markets in Guadalajara, Mazatlán, and as far north as Nogales. There were few tequila producers in those days. Like most of them, Salvador produced tequila mixto and dreamed of becoming the next Sauza or José Cuervo. A lucrative contract to make tequila for Bacardí in the 1990s meant the family didn't have to worry as much about promoting their own brand. It also allowed them to expand and renovate the distillery, adding stainless-steel fermentation vats to work alongside their existing concrete tanks and introducing a mechanical roller mill to the operation. Prior to that, agave juice had been extracted in a process combining a mechanical shredder and barefoot stomping of the fiber in a shallow tank.

Salvador Jr. ("Chava") was involved in the family business by the time the Bacardí contract ended around 2008. Chava knew that the tequila market had changed. For one thing, North Americans were starting to drink more 100% agave tequila than mixto, and many of them were actually interested in learning about the families that made tequila. During trips to the United States and Japan, it became clear to Chava that it was time to get back to basics: The family needed to build their own brand, highlight the terroir of El Arenal, and tell their story.

Over the next decade, they reintroduced more traditional methods to production: They built a tahona and created tequilas that were fermented and distilled with agave fiber. Cascahuín

had always been a respected local tequila, but the flavor explosions resulting from these "new" processes took the North American tequila world by storm. Cascahuín's arrival onto the must-have shelf of serious tequila drinkers was facilitated by their close relationship with Philadelphia restaurateur David Suro, whom Chava credits as being a catalyst for Cascahuin's return to tradition. In 2018, they collaborated to produce Siembra Valles Ancestral, the first earthen-pit-roasted tequila produced in well over a century.

DON FULANO

An uncle-nephew team that combines Highlands agave and a Valley distillery to produce sought-after tequilas from high-proof blancos to the oldest of extra-añejos.

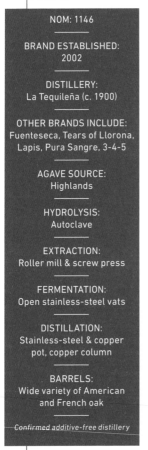

NOM: 1146

BRAND ESTABLISHED:
2002

DISTILLERY:
La Tequileña (c. 1900)

OTHER BRANDS INCLUDE:
Fuenteseca, Tears of Llorona, Lapis, Pura Sangre, 3-4-5

AGAVE SOURCE:
Highlands

HYDROLYSIS:
Autoclave

EXTRACTION:
Roller mill & screw press

FERMENTATION:
Open stainless-steel vats

DISTILLATION:
Stainless-steel & copper pot, copper column

BARRELS:
Wide variety of American and French oak

Confirmed additive-free distillery

The uncle-nephew team of Enrique Fonseca and Sergio Mendoza approach tequila making with an enthusiasm, curiosity, and playfulness that belie Fonseca's four decades in the industry. Fonseca is one of the most important agave growers in the Jalisco Highlands. He uses his agave to make tequila in Tequila, which raises the interesting and never-resolved question about whether tequilas produced at his La Tequileña distillery should be considered Valley or Los Altos products. The terroir of the agave is inarguably Highlands. But the ambient microbes and deep well water at the distillery lend the tequila earthy, herbaceous Valley characteristics. This is part of the La Tequileña mystique.

There has been a distillery on the La Tequileña site since the early 1900s. The existing distillery was built by Bacardí in the 1960s, in their first (and ultimately unsuccessful) foray into tequila making. In 1989, Fonseca bought the distillery, and Mendoza came on board around 2000. Tequileña's 12,000-square-foot layout, 40-ton autoclaves, 3,500-liter alembics, and towering column indicate it was intended to produce industrial quantities of tequila. Nevertheless, they produce small batches about four times a year.

All La Tequileña tequilas are autoclave-cooked and fermented with proprietary yeasts in 60,000- to 80,000-liter stainless-steel vats. From there, things get really interesting. Enrique uses various permutations of distilling techniques to create what he calls an "alphabet" of blancos. All-copper alembic distillation, all-stainless alembic distillation, first distillation in steel and second in copper, vice versa, and column distillation using different combinations of internal copper plates yield around sixteen different blancos, which are the building blocks for all the different La Tequileña products. Combining those sixteen base tequilas in different proportions makes possible an infinite number of blancos.

That plethora of possible blancos is multiplied by the number of possible barrel blends from Enrique's two different barrel houses, and Enrique is notably open-minded about experimenting with different barrel types and sizes. He's also pushed tequila aging past all previously accepted limits with his Fuenteseca brand. Fuenteseca has released extra-añejos aged for as long as twenty-one years.

Enrique's nephew Sergio started and runs the Don Fulano brand. Sergio is famously passionate about tequila and has eagerly absorbed his uncle's monumental knowledge of production and history. Earlier Tequileña brands like Pura Sangre, Lapis, and 3-4-5 have long been aficionado favorites, and Don Fulano has now overcome them in popularity.

Tequileña produces excellent, agave-forward blancos that appeal to purists, as well as complex, woody extra-añejos that have redefined the possibilities for aging tequila. Sergio has patiently educated thousands of aficionados and industry figures about how autoclaves and column stills—easily demonized by self-appointed traditionalists—can be carefully used to craft tequilas that stand up against any in the category.

ARETTE

The "other" family dynasty in Tequila, whose small brand has been reinvigorated by the craft cocktail movement.

NOM: 1109

BRAND ESTABLISHED:
1988

DISTILLERY:
El Llano (c. 1900)

OTHER BRANDS INCLUDE:
Arette Artesanal Suave

AGAVE SOURCE:
Tequila

HYDROLYSIS:
Autoclave, stone oven

EXTRACTION:
Roller mill

FERMENTATION:
Open stainless-steel &
concrete vats

DISTILLATION:
Stainless-steel pot

BARRELS:
Used American oak

The Orendains are the most famous and important tequileros that you have never heard of. Since the nineteenth century, they have been peers of the Cuervos and Sauzas and have played an important role in regional and industry politics. But until recently, the further away from Tequila you went, the less their name was recognized. That has begun to change with a generational shift and closer connection to the global cocktail scene.

Eduardo Orendain González was an orphan who grew up working in distilleries in the early nineteenth century. He eventually acquired land and became an important agave grower. In 1900, he bought two small adjacent distilleries in the heart of Tequila, combining them into what is now El Llano. This distillery is among the oldest still owned by a single Mexican family.

In 1970, Eduardo Orendain González's son, Jaime Orendain Hernández, bought the much larger and equally historic La Mexicana distillery and moved production of the family's house brand there. His sons Eduardo and Jaime Orendain Giovannini took over El Llano and from there launched Arette in 1988.

Jalisco is the home of charrería—Mexican rodeo—and hundreds of tequila brands have paid homage to particular horses or the species in general. Arette is named for a one-eyed Jaliscan horse that captured Mexico's national imagination in 1948, when Eduardo and Jaime were children. Army officer Humberto Mariles rode Arette to two gold medals and a bronze at the London Olympics—to date, the most golds won by a Mexican Olympian. The half-blind champion horse struck a chord in Mexico and the Orendain family, and it remains the namesake of Eduardo and Jaime's tequila.

The family modernized El Llano in the early 1980s, replacing the stone oven with autoclaves, the tahona with roller mills, and the antique copper alembics with large stainless-steel ones. They maintain high standards for agave, using their own whenever possible. The notable cooked agave notes of their blanco have long disproven the idea that such flavor can't come from autoclave production.

Arette was long the well tequila at the now-defunct San Francisco tequila bar Tres Agaves. From this initial inroad, Arette's high quality-to-price ratio saw them placed on an increasing number of cocktail menus in California. This success allowed them to sever ties with longstanding contract brands and focus exclusively on their house brands.

Unprecedented West Coast interest in Arette in turn led to more frequent visits to the distillery by American bartenders and industry figures in the 2010s. The next generation—Eduardo's son Eduardo Jr., and Jaime's sons Jaime, Alejandro, Alberto, and

Aldo—took on the lion's share of hosting responsibilities for these guests. The younger Orendains have taken note of industry preferences for more traditional methods and higher-proof tequilas. In 2017, Arette rebuilt a stone oven at El Llano to work alongside the autoclaves and soon after released a 101-proof blanco, indicating their embrace of shifting tastes.

OCHO

A seminal collaboration between two legends who introduced tequila terroir to a broad audience.

NOM: 1474

BRAND ESTABLISHED:
2007

DISTILLERY:
Los Alambiques (est. 2021)

OTHER BRANDS:
none

AGAVE SOURCE:
Highlands

HYDROLYSIS:
Stone oven

EXTRACTION:
Roller mill

FERMENTATION:
Open, wood vats

DISTILLATION:
Copper & stainless-steel pot

BARRELS:
Used American oak

Confirmed additive-free distillery

As the first single-estate tequila, Ocho changed the industry forever by laying to rest any doubts about the significance of terroir to tequila. Ocho is also the story of a special friendship between two icons of the tequila industry.

Agave farmers and traditional tequila makers have long known that tequila, like wine, exhibits terroir, or a "taste of place," depending on agave source and distillery location. But as the tequila industry grew and industrialized, the biggest producers began sourcing agave from the entire DOT region. When tequila is made with agave from all over in varying and unpredictable blends, it becomes impossible to perceive terroir. Over time the idea of terroir was de-emphasized and nearly disappeared from discussions of tequila. At best, people spoke in oversimplified terms about quintessential "Valley" and "Highlands" profiles—even as the largest producers in each region sourced agave from both areas and beyond.

In 2005, Tomás Estes and Carlos Camarena had a notion to change that, bringing agave and the idea of terroir back to the center of the tequila conversation.

A native of Los Angeles, Tomás Estes emigrated to France and would open the first tequila bars in Europe and Australia. He was eventually named the Tequila Ambassador to Europe by the National Chamber of the Tequila industry. In Europe, he became immersed in viticulture and was fascinated by the idea of terroir. On one of his frequent trips to Jalisco, he and his friend Carlos Camarena, an agronomist and renowned tequilero, began discussing how a tequila made exclusively with agave from a particular field would have a distinct taste compared to one made with agave from other fields. Thus the idea of Tequila Ocho was born.

In 2007, Ocho became the first "single-estate" tequila. Carlos produces each batch via the same process, with the same yeast, water, and equipment. But the agave for each batch comes from a particular *predio*, or piece of land, whose name and the year of production feature prominently on the label. Ocho is of consistently high quality, but the differences in aroma and flavor vary from one "vintage" to the next, and people develop strong favorites. These year-to-year differences also make Ocho a wonderful teaching tool: Even the most inexperienced taster can perceive the differences among, for example, Ocho blancos from 2015, 2016, and 2017. Those differences are exclusively an expression of terroir.

In 2020, craft spirits company Samson and Surrey acquired Ocho, leaving production in Carlos's hands. He and his three daughters run the company together, and they moved production of Ocho from La Alteña to a brand-new distillery in Arandas called Los Alambiques, which was custom-built for producing Ocho. Tomás, truly beloved throughout the industry, passed away in April 2021.

G4

The "mad scientist" of tequila who brought modern engineering to traditional production methods.

NOM: 1579

BRAND ESTABLISHED:
2013

DISTILLERY:
El Pandillo (est. 2011)

OTHER BRANDS INCLUDE:
Terralta, Volans, Primo 1861,
Don Vicente

AGAVE SOURCE:
Highlands

HYDROLYSIS:
Stone oven

EXTRACTION:
Custom mechanical "tahona"

FERMENTATION:
Open stainless-steel vats
(some with fiber), open
wooden vats

DISTILLATION:
Copper pot

BARRELS:
Used American oak

Confirmed additive-free distillery

Felipe Camarena Jr. is the eldest son of Don Felipe Camarena, the late patriarch of Tapatío and the La Alteña distillery (page 144). Hoping to establish a legacy to leave to his sons, Felipe designed, built, and inaugurated his own distillery in 2011. He called his first tequila "G4," for *"Generación Cuatro,"* his sons Luís and Alan being the fourth generation in the Camarena tequila lineage.

Felipe is trained as a mechanical engineer but is better known as the mad scientist of tequila. While "Igor and Frankenstein"— his custom-designed agave shredder and mechanical tahona built from scrap parts— get most of the attention, the entire distillery is a brilliant monument to efficiency and economy without sacrificing the quality of the tequila.

Felipe's major innovations center around energy efficiencies and highlighting the flavor effects of different water sources. His two stone ovens have escape valves that allow methanol to evaporate during cooking. This allows Felipe to take wide cuts during distillation, discarding less of the tasty heads without going over CRT thresholds and slightly increasing the total volume of tequila.

In designing his distillery, El Pandillo, Felipe applied clever engineering fixes to traditional processes, with an eye toward reducing waste. For example, he captures the hot water from the stills' condensers and uses it to preheat the mosto muerto, increasing the efficiency of distilling and lowering energy consumption. These practices may seem like obvious solutions for energy conservation, but they are nevertheless nearly unheard of in the industry.

While there is a clearly defined El Pandillo profile, the G4, Terralta, and Primo 1861 lines are distinguishable in a blind tasting. The agave source, yeast, and production techniques are the same for each line, and the sole variable is the source of water used in fermentation and dilution. G4 uses about half and half well and spring water, and bold cooked agave, black pepper, and citrus notes predominate its flavor. Terralta is made with pure well water, resulting in additional notes of minerality, earth, and an astringent mouthfeel. Primo 1861 uses only spring water, and it is subtly softer and less earthy. True to form, Felipe says he may tweak these formulas from year to year.

El Pandillo tequilas became fast favorites among aficionados because of their bold, traditional flavor profiles, their utility as teaching tools given the nuanced differences in production techniques behind each brand, and Felipe's indomitable, expansive personality.

FORTALEZA

Bringing a historic family legacy into the new millennium with showstopping flavor that helped launch the boom in artisanal tequila.

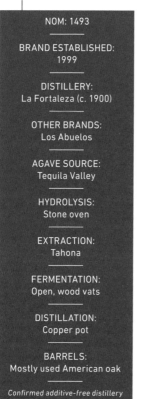

NOM: 1493

BRAND ESTABLISHED:
1999

DISTILLERY:
La Fortaleza (c. 1900)

OTHER BRANDS:
Los Abuelos

AGAVE SOURCE:
Tequila Valley

HYDROLYSIS:
Stone oven

EXTRACTION:
Tahona

FERMENTATION:
Open, wood vats

DISTILLATION:
Copper pot

BARRELS:
Mostly used American oak

Confirmed additive-free distillery

The Fortaleza ("fortitude") distillery sits within Villa Sauza near the edge of Tequila town. It was the last property Francisco Javier Sauza purchased in Tequila and the only one he kept when he sold Tequila Sauza in 1976. The Fortaleza distillery was already too antiquated for Sauza's modern techniques, and it had been mothballed for three decades when Guillermo Erickson Sauza decided to fire it up in the late 1990s.

Guillermo, the grandson of Francisco Javier, was raised in Chicago but spent his childhood summers in Tequila. He eventually became a systems engineer at IBM, and his decision to leave a successful career behind could be considered the tastiest midlife crisis in tequila history.

Fortaleza's process is in many ways a snapshot of how tequila was made in the late nineteenth century. The stone oven, pinewood fermentation vats, and all-copper alembics have all been expanded or enlarged since Fortaleza launched in 1999, but the process—including extraction done solely with a tahona—remains unchanged in essence. At the turn of the twenty-first century, Fortaleza joined a tiny handful of producers using such rustic techniques, and for a time was the only all-tahona process in the industry. Their success helped kick-start the ongoing return to artisanal methods among small tequila producers.

Fortaleza's incredible flavor, antique process, and unique family history quickly garnered it a cult following in the early 2000s. When the craft cocktail movement got wind of Fortaleza in the 2010s, the brand's sales skyrocketed. Fortaleza still enjoys a rate of growth that larger brands marvel at, and demand for their tequila frequently outstrips supply.

While most tequila brands were focused on strict flavor consistency, Fortaleza embraced the fact that seasonal changes in agave source and production resulted in recognizable variations within their distinct flavor profile. Their notably lactic blanco was sometimes naturally sweet and creamy, and at others savory, buttery, with a touch of farmhouse cheese. By hand-numbering each lot number on the bottle's back label, Fortaleza made this natural variety an intrinsic part of its brand identity. It also turns out to be great for sales, as collectors try to keep up with each new release. Fortaleza was also early to respond to purist demand for higher-proof tequila, releasing a 46% ABV "still-strength" blanco in 2017. In 2019 they began offering an annual Winter Blend of unique reposados from American and French oak.

Guillermo originally intended to produce tequila exclusively under the "Los Abuelos" label as a tribute to his forefathers, the storied "three generations" of the Sauza family (see page 140) but he was unable to do so in the United States because of a rum with a similar name. So outside of Mexico, the tequila is branded as "Fortaleza." In-country, both "Los Abuelos" and "Fortaleza" are used as brands. There is no difference in the tequila, regardless of the brand name.

LALO

The grandson of legendary tequilero Don Julio González created a blanco-only contract brand that honors his family legacy of quality tequila.

NOM: 1468

BRAND ESTABLISHED:
2020

DISTILLERY:
Grupo Tequilero México
(est. 2022)

OTHER BRANDS INCLUDE:
Alquimia, El Águila

AGAVE SOURCE:
Highlands

HYDROLYSIS:
Stone oven

EXTRACTION:
Roller mill

FERMENTATION:
Open stainless-steel vats

DISTILLATION:
Copper pot

BARRELS:
N/A

Confirmed additive-free brand

Eduardo "Lalo" González Jr. says that tequila has become confusing and that it's time to get back to basics. As the grandson of the renowned Don Julio González, Lalo knows a thing or two about tequila. Don Julio founded the La Primavera distillery in 1942 and, in 1989, his namesake tequila, which the family later sold. A few years after that, Lalo saw his uncles build their own distillery and launch the Reserva de los González brand.

Reserva was successful in Jalisco but never caught on anywhere else. Lalo says he learned a valuable lesson from his family's experience with Reserva: Having excellent tequila is no guarantee of success, and like it or not, branding and packaging matter a great deal.

Lalo's childhood friend David R. Carballido approached him about creating a private-label tequila for friends and family in Jalisco. David was behind the wildly successful Guadalajara marketing of Don Julio 70, one of the first cristalino tequilas (see page 61). This was somewhat ironic, as Lalo wasn't a fan of the cristalino boom. He saw the style of clear-filtered aged tequilas as confusing to consumers and part of a dilution of authenticity and tradition in tequila. If he was going to get into the family business, it was going to be with a clean, natural tequila, made with the goal of "honoring the agave."

The two friends decided to work with a well-known Arandas distillery, Grupo Tequilero México, to make their tequila. They knew they wanted a blanco tequila made with mature Highlands agave that was oven cooked and additive free. They eventually settled on a Champagne yeast that gave them the agave-forward profile they were looking for.

When Lalo's father (also named Eduardo "Lalo" González) passed away in 2017, he didn't want the family legacy to die with his dad, so he changed the name of the brand to Lalo, in honor of his father. The Lalo bottle also features other subtle tributes. It is short and stout, a shape that grandfather Don Julio pioneered, so that people could see each other over the tequila bottles on the dinner table. The blue and gold on the neck label evoke Jalisco's state flag, and the label and cap feature the iconic San Francisco de Asís church in the family's hometown of Atotonilco el Alto.

Lalo launched in Texas in 2020 and quickly became one of the fastest-selling tequilas in the state. Eduardo and his partners plan to expand to other parts of the United States and eventually to Mexico. He points out that this reflects the reality that the United States is a bigger market for premium, 100% agave tequila than Mexico. He looks forward to making Lalo available in Mexico, and in the meantime is committed to "honoring the family legacy in a serious way."

THE OUTLIERS
When Tequila Is Not Tequila

The Denomination of Origin for Tequila (DOT) is supposed to protect and support the communities where tequila was born. In the first twenty-five years of Tequila Regulatory Council (CRT) oversight (1995–2021), tequila exports more than quadrupled, and foreign pseudo-tequila was stamped out as a serious threat. In those terms, the system has been successful. But the benefits haven't been shared equally, and some of the most traditional tequileros have never been part of the official tequila system. Some, arguably, have been excluded intentionally. Others have decided to forgo using the name "tequila" and have opted out of the system voluntarily.

THE EXCLUDED
Traditional Taverneros

▸▸▸▸▸▸▸▸▸

The municipality of Tequila includes communities in the Santiago River gorge and the imposing mountain range to the north. Down by the river and up in the sierra, an unknown number of traditional *taverneros* eke out a living farming and occasionally distilling a liquor from blue agave that can't legally be called tequila. Despite being stewards of traditional tequila production methods, these folks have never been invited to the official tequila party.

One of them, Alfredo Ríos, lives with his family in a simple, tidy house at the end of a treacherous road in the high sierra above Tequila town. In the sixteenth century, this was the seat of local government and a thriving mining town. It is also one of the cradles of the tradition that we now know as tequila.

This is apparent in the local lingo—the blue agave is "mezcal," which is *"tatemado"* (roasted), *"machucado"* (crushed), fermented in *pipas*, and distilled into *vino* at the family *taverna* (distillery) in a wood-fired copper alembic that belonged to Alfredo's grandfather. From the time that he "could carry heavy loads," about age fifteen, Alfredo helped his dad produce vino. "My father taught us to make good, clean tequila—no tricks. And it became kinda famous around here." Rios's children now help in the taverna after school.

Traditional taverneros are the stuff of dioramas and historical reenactments in Tequila town. Any tour guide on the town plaza will tell you that there are no more real tavernas. Legally, there's something to that. People like Alfredo don't show up on tax rolls, and their tavernas are uncertified. Their booze can't officially be sold as tequila, much less exported to the lucrative US market. Their primitive techniques also yield far less per kilo of agave than commercial processes. This traditional vino could never be made nearly as cheaply as other tequila, even before adding Mexico's crushing 70% tax on liquor.

Although Alfredo's community has been profiled in an industry-sponsored documentary on tequila's origins, he says they've never been approached by the CRT about becoming certified and joining the industry. This is also the case for his brothers, neighbors, and other taverneros in the sierra of Tequila and the Río Santiago gorge below.

Tequilero Alfredo Ríos at his taverna in Tequila, Jalisco.

THE OPT-OUTS
Caballito Cerrero

● ● ● ● ● ● ● ● ● ●

Caballito Cerrero is also not officially tequila. The brand was known as a legendary tequila for more than fifty years, praised for its excellent quality and the legacy of the family that makes it. But it has never been a part of the CRT system, and since 2019 it has been labeled as an "agave distillate" rather than a tequila. Its very existence is an implicit critique of the tequila regulatory system and the Denomination of Origin and possibly a harbinger of increasing dissatisfaction with both.

Javier Jiménez Sr. and his family produce Caballito Cerrero in Amatitán's Tecuane gorge. Their family's roots in vino mezcal go back to the seventeenth century, and their property includes the oldest confirmed site of distillation in Jalisco. The Jiménezes make Caballito Cerrero at the Santa Rita distillery on the same land. The distillery was state of the art when it was built in 1873, with top-loading stone ovens, roller mills, in-ground fermentation pits, copper-pot alembics, and a small train to move cooked agave from oven to mill. These days, fermentation happens in stainless-steel tanks, and the train is just a monument to the past, but the process is otherwise unchanged. The result is a delicious, agave- and anise-forward Valley "tequila" that is still bottled the "old-school" way at 46% ABV.

Tequila Caballito Cerrero was immediately a favorite of Guadalajara tequila drinkers when it was introduced in 1950. As the tequila Norm became more permissive, Caballito Cerrero was one of a small handful of brands that maintained traditional production of 100% agave tequila. By the time the CRT was created in 1994, the local market for authentic tequila was small, and Caballito's tiny production volume was all sold at the Jiménez family's cantina. The nascent CRT had the massive falsification of tequila in other countries to contend with, and Caballito's use of the "tequila" label without certification

Opposite page: Tequilero and Caballito Cerrero owner Javier Jiménez Sr. at his distillery in Amatitán, Jalisco.

was not on their radar. By the turn of the century, Caballito Cerrero was an elusive treasure and had achieved a mythical "outlaw" reputation among foreign aficionados.

By 2017, Javier Jr. had become more centrally involved in the family business. He saw what was happening in the United States: The mezcal boom was helping drive consumers' search for authentic tequilas with a real connection to specific places and histories. Those consumers were also willing to pay what it actually cost to produce a quality product. He and his father decided it was time to bring Caballito Cerrero out of the shadows and to the US market for the first time.

After testing the waters of CRT certification, the Javiers decided that opting out of the DOT was the best way to uphold the tequila traditions that their family had maintained for centuries. Staying outside of the system kept them free of institutional pressure to increase the efficiency of their process, shielded them from tequila industry politics, and allowed them to use traditional agave varietals that have been prohibited by the tequila Norm since 1964.

Caballito Cerrero officially became an "agave distillate," and the Jiménezes bet that the brand's reputation and quality could stand on its own, without the "tequila" name. That gamble is paying off, big time. In 2019, Caballito Cerrero launched in the United States, with an $80 retail price for a 750 ml bottle of blanco: twice what many good certified tequilas sell for. The brand's status as a *destilado* also allows them to sell a blanco made from the agave subvarietal *chato*. The first batch quickly sold out, at nearly $200 a bottle. Caballito's early success in the United States and Canada has aroused the attention of other brands, and it may be only a matter of time before other quality tequilas opt out of the DOT system and become agave distillates.

CHAPTER 4

EXPERIENCING
TEQUILA

TASTING, HOSTING, AND VISITING THE TEQUILA REGION

WHAT'S THE BEST WAY TO ENJOY TEQUILA?

Tequila should be sipped, savored, and shared. Tequila is also a physical place, one that can be visited, appreciated, and absorbed.

The world of tequila tasting can seem intimidating at first. The lingo, special glassware, and little rituals make it seem like some kind of exclusive club. But the basics of tequila tasting are simple, and all that's required to become a skilled taster is practice and a few basic tools.

Tequila is best when shared. It has a power to bring people together, and even professional tasters prefer sharing tequila to sipping alone, hunched over their notes. Hosting a formal tasting and sharing tequila knowledge with friends doesn't have to be complicated. Preparation, organization, and attention to detail are all that is required to blow minds and dazzle palates.

Most tequila will eventually find its way into cocktails, and this has been the most popular way of consuming tequila for decades. Even if you prefer your tequila neat, a few basic cocktails are an undeniable part of tequila culture, and it's worthwhile to learn how to make them well.

Most people find that their tequila tasting journey eventually leads to Jalisco and to the valley and village of Tequila itself. Tequila travel has become easier than ever in recent years, and it's possible to put together an agave pilgrimage on just about any budget. There are, however, some definite dos and don'ts as well as some hard-won advice in this chapter that will help make your tequila trip a success.

Opposite page: Tequila's iconic sixteenth-century church, the Parroquia Santiago Apóstol, located in the town center.

TASTING VS. DRINKING

Tasting and drinking are both great ways of enjoying tequila, but they aren't synonymous and should be done in the correct order. There is no wrong way to drink tequila, provided you're not harming yourself or infringing on anyone else. Tasting is different. There are plenty of wrong ways to taste tequila, and really only one way to taste tequila properly.

We drink, primarily, for pleasure. Perhaps we drink to unwind after a long day or to loosen up at a social event, but in any case, we drink to alter our mood. Basics like knowing our limits, eating, hydrating, not driving, and seeking help if we have a problem all need to be kept in mind with regard to drinking. But otherwise, there is no right or wrong way to do it.

Tasting, on the other hand, is work. While tasting the right spirit can certainly bring pleasure, we must be meticulous in our approach to tasting. Treating tasting as work will bring you more pleasure later, when you are drinking, because you will have learned to select the most appropriate tequilas for your individual palate and for the occasion.

The distinction between drinking and tasting is a bit like the difference between dancing at a party and training in ballet. Professional dancers certainly enjoy their art. But it involves a lot of hard work that often, at any given moment, is not especially carefree.

BLIND TASTING

Scientific studies of wine drinkers show that just about everyone is influenced by labels, and the same applies to tequila. We can't help but develop preconceptions that a product will be good or bad based on what the bottle looks like, how much it costs, what our friends or experts say about it, and so on.

Blind tasting is the only way to correct for those biases and to get a true sense of what you actually think about a tequila. Tasting blind as much as possible will make you a better taster, teach you more about your own preferences, and keep you honest.

You will need someone to help you taste blind; unfortunately, it's impossible to do it alone. Simply have your helper pour one or more tequilas into tasting glasses out of your view, making sure to keep careful track of which is which. Labeling tasting glasses with a dry erase marker with numbers or letters that correspond to the hidden bottles is a good way to avoid confusion.

Blind tasting can lead to surprises, and you may find that you don't actually like your favorite as much as you thought, or that a budget sipper that you turned your nose up at is much better than you realized.

Opposite page: A mural in Tequila's main plaza welcomes visitors from all over the world.

TEQUILA TASTING DOS AND DON'TS

The whole point of making tequila is consuming it, of course. With thousands of brands on the market, choosing tequila can be overwhelming. The best way to zero in on the tequilas that are right for you is by taking tasting seriously. Tasting tequila gives perspective on which ones you like, which ones you don't like, and why. From there, you can go on to enjoying tequila in cocktails or on the rocks, or continue sipping it neat. Even though tasting looks fun, it can be hard work that requires sustained focus and challenges the senses. But developing the skills to taste tequila properly will make relaxed tequila drinking more enjoyable later.

- Taste at a consistent time of day, preferably early

- Eat bland food beforehand

- Stay hydrated

- Pour enough to smell the tequila (½ to 1 ounce)

- Keep a record of your notes and evaluations

- Taste blind when possible

- Eat spicy, sweet, sour, bitter, or highly flavorful food

- Feel compelled to drink the whole sample

- Wear cologne, perfume, lotion, or any products with a strong fragrance

- Talk with others or compare notes while tasting

HOW TO TASTE TEQUILA

Most people choose a tequila based on marketing or word-of-mouth recommendation. But taste preferences are highly individual, and you are the single best judge of which tequilas taste best to you. There are a lot of stereotypes and received wisdom in the tequila world: "Valley tequilas are spicy and Highlands tequilas are fruity," "oven-cooked tequilas are more agave-forward than autoclave tequilas," "tahona tequilas have a lot of minerality," and things like that. In a tasting, such statements are just as likely to be contradicted as verified, and what's true for one taster may not be for another. It's crucial to develop some basic tasting skills so that you can trust your own mouth

SENSORY PERCEPTION

When you are using all five of your senses, your brain cannot focus on any one of them as well as it can when individually isolated. This is why we reflexively close our eyes when listening intently to a piece of music or turn off the car radio when we are trying to parallel park. When tasting tequila, you want to focus on your senses of smell, taste, and (to a lesser degree) touch. The more you can diminish visual and auditory input, the easier it will be to taste. Tasting alone in a quiet room will yield better results than in a crowded bar. Closing your eyes when you taste will allow your brain to focus on aromas and flavors.

After tasting several tequilas, your olfactory sense may become fatigued. The tequilas may all start to smell the same, or you may begin to wonder if you are imagining aromas out of boredom. There is one tried and true way to recalibrate your sense of smell. Hold your inner wrist or forearm up to your nose and take a good long inhale. The smell of your own skin is a natural baseline, and after doing this "reset," tequila aromas should "pop" again.

and make your own judgments about the qualities and the quality of any given tequila.

Knowing what to look for and using a shared tasting vocabulary are helpful. By practicing these tasting techniques, you will be able to parse out specific characteristics of appearance, aroma, flavor, mouthfeel, and finish. This learning process never ends, and by tasting as many different tequilas as possible over time, you will continuously improve your ability to distinguish the elements of tequila.

1. VISUAL ANALYSIS

The first step to tasting tequila is to look at the spirit, both to appreciate it and to scan for flaws. Don't spend too much time here, though: Visual flaws in tequila are rare these days, and people who spend a

CLARITY is the quality of being clear. Unaged tequilas are transparent, and rested or aged tequilas are translucent (cristalinos notwithstanding). If the tequila is cloudy or contains specks, that is a flaw that should be noted.

BRILLIANCE is the degree to which the tequila sparkles. It can be hard to tell that it does, but if you compare it to water in the same type of glass, you will notice the difference.

COLOR ranges from perfectly clear to the color of pale straw to various shades of gold into amber.

BODY refers to the tequila's thickness or density. This is the visual component that varies the most. Give the tequila a gentle swirl around the glass. Observe how a "crown" forms near the top and how "legs" or "tears" run down the glass. Comparing many different tequilas will help you calibrate what is a light or thin body, compared to a medium body, as opposed to a grand body.

long time gazing at their upraised glass are usually just trying to show off.

You're analyzing the tequila's visual aspect along four dimensions: clarity, brilliance, color, and body. Hold your glass against a well-lit white background—a wall, tablecloth, napkin, or tasting mat—when analyzing these elements.

2. THE WARM-UP

The warm-up is one of the most important practices to become a better taster and to ultimately enjoy tequila more. The warm-up cleans out your mouth, wakes up your taste buds, and allows the initial shocking "bite" of the first sip to pass before you start making judgments about the tequila.

Take a very small amount of tequila into your mouth. Really, the smallest volume that can still reasonably be called a sip. You are going to use that tiny bit of tequila to warm up your palate. First, use your tongue to rub the tequila into your upper gums. Next, do the same with your lower gums. Then, rub the tequila into the hard palate on the roof of your mouth. Go ahead and swallow whatever is left, but do not think too much about your reaction to the tequila. Whether positive, negative, or indifferent, it's just part of warming up. You are not tasting yet!

The first few times you warm up, it will be quite intense. After all, you don't rub liquor onto your sensitive mucous membranes for enjoyment. Remember, tasting is work, and this warm-up is as necessary (and potentially unpleasant) as the one you would do before an intense physical workout. Your mouth may burn, tingle, or even seem to vibrate. Congratulations: Your mouth is wide awake, and your taste buds are ready to go!

Feel free to take a drink of water if you like after warming up. Always drink as much water as you want when you are tasting. The warm-up need only be done once in any single tasting session. If you take a break and have some food, do more than one tasting in a day, or move into higher-proof tequilas, you should repeat the warm-up. Once you are warmed up, you are ready to taste.

3. TASTING

Having warmed up your palate with a tiny sip, your next tiny sip will be the beginning of the actual tasting. Using your breath correctly is crucial to tasting. Before you take a sip, make sure that your lungs are filled with air. Beginners should take an exaggerated inhale before each sip to get into the habit. With practice, this will all become second nature.

While holding your breath in, take another sip of tequila as small as the one in your warm-up. This time, gently roll it across your tongue from front to back three times: back, forth, and back again. Make sure that the entire surface of your tongue is coated with tequila. Then, gently swallow.

After swallowing, gently exhale through your mouth. This exhale is where the real tasting happens, as the volatile vapors pass over your tastebuds and through your nasal passages. The flavors should really bloom and become apparent.

Some tasters exhale through their nose rather than the mouth, although most people find that to be overly intense or even painful. If you like, try it once after you've got the hang of exhaling through the mouth. If you are one of the few who prefer to exhale through your nose, then by all means, do so.

If you've warmed up properly, you should notice something important on your first taste (which is your second sip). While the tequila's ABV hasn't changed, your perception of the alcohol should be lower, allowing you to better perceive and focus on aromas and flavors. Many beginning tasters perceive this as the tequila being "smoother," or burning less, after warming up the palate. The tequila is the same, but the warm-up changes your perception, sharpening your focus on aroma and flavor.

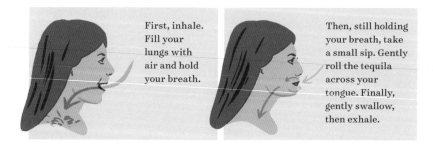

First, inhale. Fill your lungs with air and hold your breath.

Then, still holding your breath, take a small sip. Gently roll the tequila across your tongue. Finally, gently swallow, then exhale.

4. AROMA/NOSE

You probably haven't been able to avoid smelling or "nosing" the tequila as you tasted it. Now it's time to do it deliberately.

It's important to use a glass with plenty of empty space (i.e., air) in it because you are going to tilt the glass significantly, forming about a 30-degree angle to the ground. This lets the tequila spread out along the side of the glass, increasing its surface area and allowing more aroma to escape.

Tequila should be aromatically complex, so there are a variety of different gases—perceived as aromas—evaporating at different rates, based on their molecular weight. When you hold a glass vertically, your nose will be hit first by the most volatile (fastest to evaporate) and aromatically least interesting element: alcohol.

Holding the glass at an extreme tilt allows that boring alcohol aroma to escape, up to the top of the glass. You're going to start "nosing" at the bottom, where heavier primary aromas tend to hang out. These aromas will often be ones associated with the raw material, cooking, and extraction: raw and cooked agave, stone, earth, cut grass, and so on.

TASTING BEFORE NOSING?

Most people are used to the idea of nosing before tasting. This is common practice for tasting wine and other spirits. But because most of us are not savants or naturally gifted tasters, tasting before nosing is more efficient for most people. For inexperienced tasters, the first pass at nosing often yields little information. After warming up the palate and tasting, a second pass at aromas turns up more. That first pass can be frustrating, and you can waste a lot of time if you have many samples to get through. So go straight to warming up the palate, tasting, and then return to nosing the glass before moving on to finish. Once you've built your confidence as an experienced taster, go ahead and try the other way, nosing before tasting. If that ultimately works for you, then by all means, reverse steps three and four.

The middle of the glass—the widest part of the opening—is where we tend to find the multitudinous secondary aromas: fruit, flowers, herbs, and spices. Up near the top of the glass, you'll usually perceive alcohol (in blancos) or tertiary notes from oak (in rested and aged tequilas).

If you find parsing out those different zones challenging (or if this just sounds like a bunch of malarkey), try this: Close your eyes while holding your glass at that 30-degree tilt. Part your lips slightly. Start with your nose at the bottom of the glass—the tip of it may even rest on the lip of the glass. Inhale gently and consistently as you move your nose from the bottom to the top of the glass, smoothly and evenly, over the course of the inhalation. As you do this, you should notice a distinct difference between aromas at the bottom and at the top. Once you've noticed that difference, do it again, even slower and with more focus. Try to distinguish the bottom, middle, and top. When you can do that, you are well on your way to being able to perceive dozens of aromas.

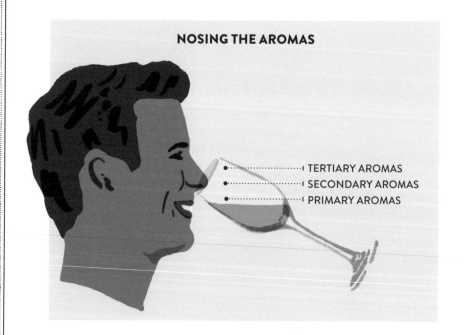

NOSING THE AROMAS

TERTIARY AROMAS
SECONDARY AROMAS
PRIMARY AROMAS

5. FINISH

After nosing, you'll need to take one more small sip to evaluate finish and mouthfeel. How a tequila finishes is the final element in a tasting, and it is crucial to describing its overall profile and quality.

When evaluating the finish, focus on three elements: the length of the finish, the mouthfeel, and any changes that occur on the palate after swallowing. The length of a tequila's finish is straightforward, and beginners should even consider using a timer to record how long it takes for the flavors and sensations to dissipate from the mouth. Anything under ten seconds is a short finish, and anything over thirty seconds is a long finish. All things being equal, aged tequila will have a longer finish than a blanco.

The term "mouthfeel" means just what it sounds like: how the tequila feels in your mouth. Part of this is body—tequila may be "thin" and leave no physical remnant. At the other extreme, it may be full-bodied, even unctuous. Texture is another element. Think of a continuum from the smooth feel of silk to the sensation of rubbing velvet against the grain. The latter, rougher texture is another way of describing astringency, which typically leaves your mouth feeling dry. None of these descriptors are necessarily pejorative, with the possible exception of "thin." What may be enjoyably full-bodied to you might feel overly oily to the next taster. While some people find almost any degree of astringency to be a flaw, others enjoy the sensation to a point. These physical sensations form an important part of the tequila's character or personality. These elements can help you determine which tequilas are appropriate for which settings.

Other sensations may include mild menthol-like numbness or tingling. Some tequilas may even leave a film in your mouth and on your teeth. For serious tasting notes, try to avoid value judgments and stick to description, unless particular aromas, flavors, or sensations are remarkably unpleasant (e.g., sulfur, wet dog, metallic, etc.).

AROMA AND FLAVOR

To a beginner, offering tasting notes can feel intimidating. Others may let loose a litany of poetic descriptors, including unfamiliar or questionable references (quince? white pepper? green papaya? wet cement?). Meanwhile, a beginner may feel more comfortable with comments like "smells and tastes like tequila—yum!"

KEEPING TRACK OF TASTING NOTES

If you get serious about tasting, you'll quickly realize that a system for maintaining a record of your tasting notes and reviews is crucial.

How do you make tasting notes and keep track of them all? Pencil and paper, spreadsheets, or Cloud-based documents work just fine for some people. But the best tool for tracking tasting notes is the Tequila Matchmaker app. The app has become as indispensable as a Riedel tasting glass for industry professionals and aficionados and connects more than 200,000 users worldwide. Matchmaker regularly updates its database of all 100% agave tequilas, and the app prompts you for ratings on aroma, flavor, finish, and value. You can add written notes on appearance, choose from hundreds of possible aromas and flavors, and add your own. There is also a feature for tasting tequilas blind, which allows you to attach your review to the appropriate tequila once it is revealed to you.

The app will keep a handy record of your tastings, show you how others (including a panel of experts) rate the same tequilas, and make your ratings and notes publicly visible if you choose. The more you rate, the better the app gets at predicting your tastes and recommending tequilas you might like based on your reviews.

A lot of the people producing elaborate tasting notes are just making that stuff up. But those who aren't bluffing have usually been tasting seriously for years. They have mastered the art of discerning aromas and flavors through the only way of getting good at anything: practice, practice, practice.

The first question when parsing aroma and flavor is "How present is the agave?" Because all tequila is made primarily from agave and serious tasting generally focuses on 100% agave tequila, agave should be present in smell and taste. It will likely be more pronounced in blancos than in other classes of tequila. The experience of tasting cooked agave at a tequila distillery is fundamental in centering the palate on tequila's primary ingredient. If you're not able to do that yet, taste some of the commercially available agave syrup (often sold as "nectar") in stores. Those syrups don't taste exactly like cooked agave, but they are very close. If you can't get your hands on agave syrup, bake a yam in the oven until it starts to ooze caramelized juice. That juice is also close to what cooked agave tastes like.

Once you've determined whether the tequila has no, slight, moderate, or strong agave aroma and flavor, move on to the super-categories of fruit, floral, herb, and spice. How fruity is the tequila? How floral? How herbal, how spicy? When you're starting out, answering these questions may be as far as you can go.

But with time and practice, you will start to zero in on specific notes that you perceive within the super-categories. It's not just moderately fruity, but it's citric with a touch of banana on the finish. It's not just slightly floral but has the aroma of orange blossoms. Herbal tequilas reveal the aroma and flavor of mint and anise, and spicy ones taste like black pepper or cinnamon. Don't be afraid to be honest and use your own words. Remember that there is an objective, chemical basis for the aromas and flavors found in tequila and some are much more common than others. Learning to identify them helps contribute to a common vocabulary used among tasters.

AROMA AND FLAVOR WHEEL

This tool features some of the most common aromas and flavors found in tequila. Use it to help you identify and parse out aromas in different parts of the glass.

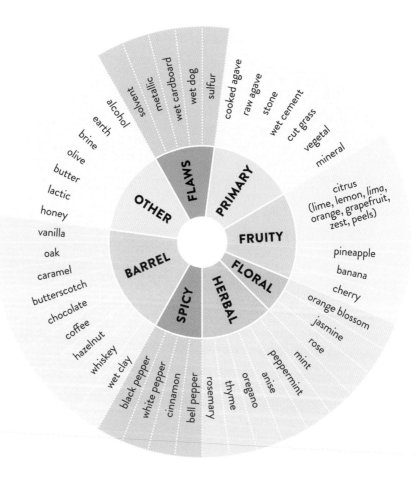

GLASSWARE MATTERS

Tasting techniques vary little between spirits categories, but glassware can be quite specific. Cognac snifters and Glencairns (for Scotch) are well-known examples of specialized glassware used for specific categories of spirits. For tequila, the Riedel Ouverture is the semi-official tasting glass, although there are other acceptable options. The Ouverture was developed by the legendary Austrian crystal maker in collaboration with the National Chamber of the Tequila Industry (CNIT). It is preferred by most tequila experts in Mexico and abroad. Nevertheless, Riedels are both expensive and fragile. A simple Champagne flute is nearly as good for most tasters on most occasions. Other options include wine glasses and snifters. Even a good old rocks glass will do in a pinch. The key is to experiment, pick a type of glassware, and stick with it.

When you're a guest at a bar, restaurant, or someone's home, you don't always have the luxury of using your preferred glassware. But whenever possible, use the same type of glassware every time you evaluate tequila. This will make your tasting scores and evaluations comparable and more meaningful, as the form of the glass has a remarkable effect on aroma and flavor.

If you have doubts about the importance of glassware, try the following exercise: Pour one to two ounces of the same tequila into a variety of glasses. Include a Riedel or flute, a snifter, a rocks glass, a standard North American shot glass, and a Mexican *caballito*. Use the same tequila in each glass! Nose each glass, writing down all your perceptions for each. Remember that perception doesn't just mean aroma. How does the glass feel in your hand? Does your lip get wet? Which options maximize your ability to discern different aromas in the glass?

This exercise can be mind-blowing when done blind. Even industry professionals often insist that each glass contains a different tequila. The shape of each glass will emphasize different aspects of the same tequila, some making it seem "smoother" or sweeter to the nose, others concentrating alcohol vapor, making the tequila seem harsh and hot. Shot glasses of any type, for example, make it difficult to perceive any aroma other than alcohol. They're impossible to move around to nose for other aromas, which is why they are never an appropriate choice for tasting tequila. The glassware really does matter.

- Use the same type of glass for each sample

- Wash glasses with hot water and fragrance-free soap

- Thoroughly rinse off all soap residue

- Allow glasses to drip dry and then polish them with a microfiber cloth

- Use shot glasses for tasting

- Dry glasses with paper or terry cloth towels

- Feel that you need expensive glassware to taste

GLASSES FOR TASTING TEQUILA

RIEDEL OUVERTURE   ROCKS GLASS   SNIFTER   WINE GLASS   FLUTE

GLASSES NOT FOR TASTING TEQUILA

CABALLITO   SHOT GLASS

TASTING FLIGHTS

Tequila tastings are commonly arranged as "flights," a term borrowed from the wine world. The most basic types of flights are vertical and horizontal, but the concept is flexible enough to allow for limitless creativity in selecting tequilas. In general, flights start with the least aged tequila and progress to the most aged.

Flights usually consist of at least three tequilas and may extend to several dozen in tasting competitions. Six tequilas is a good limit for most tastings. In competitions, judges spit out each tequila after sampling it to stay sober (see Tequila Tasting Competitions, page 204). During social tastings, most people won't want to spit. Swallowing at least some of each sample is necessary to evaluate finish, but overdoing it can make for an unpleasant experience, of course. Palate fatigue is another reason to choose a reasonable upper limit on the number of tequilas you serve. Untrained tasters will typically start to tire after intensely focusing on perceiving and describing aroma and flavor after about six samples. If you are serving half-ounce tastes of six tequilas, each person will consume three ounces of tequila—the equivalent of about two cocktails. You'll want to provide snacks and water to help the tasters moderate their alcohol consumption.

Taste the tequilas one at a time. Take your time tasting each one, observing your reactions, making notes, and discussing each tequila with fellow tasters.

VERTICAL FLIGHTS. A vertical flight is a tasting that progresses from the least to the most aged tequila. A basic vertical flight may consist of a single brand. For example, a tasting of Herradura tequilas, ordered as blanco, reposado, añejo, and extra-añejo is a classic vertical flight. This allows you to taste the evolution of the brand as it spends more time in oak barrels.

You want to avoid going backward in a vertical flight. The oaky notes of an añejo or extra-añejo can make even an excellent blanco seem harsh, flat, or insipid by contrast.

With vertical flights, feel free to nose the different samples as many times as you like. However, tasting itself should be done in one direction only, taking time to make thorough notes on the blanco before moving on to the reposado, and so on down the line.

HORIZONTAL FLIGHTS. A horizontal flight is a tasting of multiple tequilas within the same class. For example, you might want to explore the reposado class by comparing how different barrel types and aging times are expressed in Tres Generaciones, Pueblo Viejo, Viva México, and Don Fulano reposados. As long as all the samples are the same ABV, you can both taste and nose back and forth within the flight.

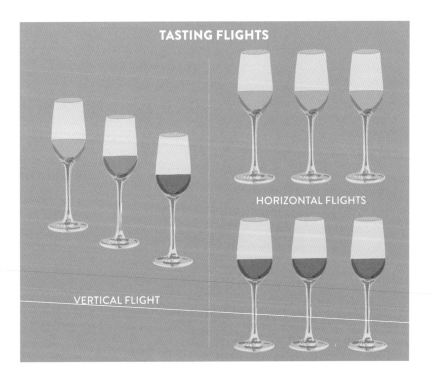

TASTING FLIGHTS

HORIZONTAL FLIGHTS

VERTICAL FLIGHT

ADVANCED FLIGHTS. You can also create a vertical tasting using tequilas from a mix of different brands. A mixed vertical flight is a great way to quickly demonstrate the potential breadth of the tequila category. For example, you could taste a mixed vertical flight of Cascahuín blanco, Don Fulano reposado, Fortaleza añejo, and Don Abraham extra-añejo.

Increasing the level of complexity slightly, a paired vertical tasting compares two different lines of tequila, such as Fortaleza blanco, Siete Leguas blanco, Fortaleza repo, Siete Leguas repo, Fortaleza añejo, and Siete Leguas añejo. In this way, you can compare how two distinct lines evolve in the barrel.

A paired, mixed vertical combines the previous two options and does the simultaneous work of showing how a tequila evolves in the barrel as well as the potential breadth of the tequila category by comparing, say, G4 blanco, Lalo blanco, G4 reposado, Patrón reposado, G4 añejo, and Don Abraham añejo.

Any of these types of flights can be organized to highlight themes of region or production method. For example, a paired vertical flight could compare a brand that uses exclusively Valley agave with one that uses exclusively Highland agave, or it could compare a diffuser tequila with an oven-and-tahona tequila.

The possibilities are infinite when you begin to consider "scatter-shot" flights, which include as many as six different brands. These flights can be designed around a theme or simply picked to include as much diversity of aroma and flavor as possible.

HOSTING A TEQUILA TASTING

One of the most fun ways to build and share your tequila knowledge is to host a tequila tasting. This can be done formally or informally, and there are only a few key things to keep in mind to make your tasting a success.

CHOOSE YOUR TEQUILAS WITH CARE. Decide if you are doing a vertical or horizontal flight and take particular care to put the tequilas in the best order possible: from least to most aged for a vertical flight or lowest to highest ABV for a horizontal flight (see page 195).

USE APPROPRIATE GLASSWARE. Ideally, each tequila in a flight is served in the same type of glass and each participant has their own set of glasses. If you have three tequilas and ten guests, that's thirty-three glasses (don't forget yourself!). That's more glassware than most people keep on hand and can create a lot of extra cleanup. Glassware can be rented, but unless you are in a wine region, be aware that you may need to wash the glasses before the tasting to remove any residual soap. If you're going to start hosting tastings regularly, it's probably worth investing in your own glassware. Remember, glassware doesn't need to be fancy, it just needs to be consistent. Look for Champagne flutes at dollar stores in December when they're stocked for the holidays. If you diligently wash and dry your glasses after each tasting, wrap them in tissue paper, and store them in sealed boxes, they should be ready to go for your next tasting after a quick polish with a microfiber cloth.

PROVIDE PLENTY OF WATER AND APPROPRIATE SNACKS. If water is present and plentiful, people will drink it. If it isn't, they may not remember to ask for it in the excitement of the tasting. Regular hydration during a tasting will go a long way toward your guests feeling great the next day. Saltines or water crackers; bread; mild, soft cheeses (such as Munster or panela); and peanuts make ideal snacks to graze on while waiting for a tasting to begin. Offering a hearty meal once the tasting is finished is always a great idea.

BE ORGANIZED. If you really want to impress your guests with how sophisticated and flavorful tequila can be, focus on curating a small, thoughtful tasting flight instead of overwhelming guests with a large variety of different tequilas. For your first flight, consider tasting only three or four.

HOW TO ORGANIZE A FORMAL TASTING

In a proper tequila tasting, each guest's complete flight is pre-poured and ready for them when they arrive. Good organization is key to a successful tasting. Confusing which tequila is in which glass can ruin an otherwise well-planned event, so it is worth taking the time to organize your tequilas and glassware properly.

Preparing a tequila tasting is a skill that improves with practice, so give yourself plenty of extra time when you're new to it. There's a balance between allowing tequila to breathe in the glasses for a bit and overexposing it to oxygen by letting it sit too long before tasting. For your first few tastings, setting things up will take longer than you expect, and you should err on the side of being ready early. Ideally, the final tequila will be set in its covered glass twenty or thirty minutes before the tasting starts, but allowing as many as ninety minutes between the final pour and first taste won't hurt the tequila—and you'll be a more relaxed, better organized host if you allow yourself a little more time to prepare.

SET UP YOUR SPACE. You'll need a tasting table where your guests will sample the tequilas, and a separate clean, open space to use as a staging area where you will organize your glassware and pour the tequila samples before placing them on the tasting table.

PLACE A TASTING MAT FOR EACH GUEST AT THE TASTING TABLE. Tasting mats are sheets of paper that are used like place mats. They are marked with spaces to indicate where each tequila will be placed on the mat, and they may include distillery and production information if it isn't a blind tasting.

CREATE "BLOCKS." Before pouring any tequila, organize your glassware into "blocks," or groups, for each spirit to be tasted. Each block

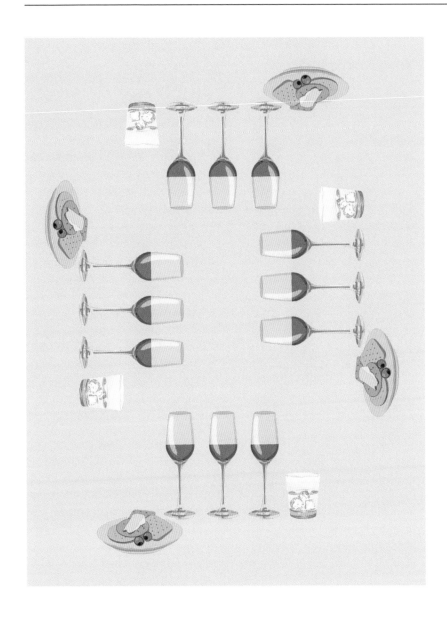

will have a glass for each guest. For example, if you have four people tasting a flight of three tequilas, you'll need to make three blocks of four glasses. For a group of six people tasting five tequilas, make five blocks of six glasses, and so on.

POUR. To ensure consistency and avoid mistakes, you'll pour all the samples of each tequila one at a time, each into its own block, before moving on to the next tequila. Use a measuring pour, jigger, or control spout to ensure the same amount of tequila is in each glass. For flights of three or four tequilas, ¾ of an ounce to 1 ounce is a good amount. For tastings with five or more tequilas, half an ounce of each tequila is best. Unless your guests are very experienced spirits tasters, serving less than half an ounce will make it very challenging to parse out aromas. Tasters should be reminded that they don't need to finish all the tequila in their glass!

Pour the most-aged tequila first. For example, in a basic vertical flight of three tequilas (a blanco, a reposado, and an añejo) the añejo is poured first. This is the reverse of the order the tequilas will be tasted, but aged tequilas can tolerate more time in contact with oxygen than blancos.

Repeat this process for the reposado and then the blanco. Once you have three nicely organized blocks of glasses, you are ready to place the glasses on the mats. Place all the añejos, followed by the reposados, and then the blancos. You should never bring out more than one type of tequila from the staging area to the tasting mats at the same time.

COVER THE GLASSES. If you'd like, you can top your glasses with glass, plastic, or laminated paper caps to cover each glass. Toppers are not essential, but they improve tastings in three ways. First, they inhibit evaporation and retain aroma in the glass. They also discourage guests from getting started early or moving from one tequila to another before the host is ready. Finally, glass toppers can contribute to the elegant look of a tasting. If you don't want to invest in glass toppers, you can always use napkins or nice paper to cover the tequilas until you are ready to taste.

Opposite page: A blind, vertical tequila tasting flight.

TEQUILA TASTING COMPETITIONS

Tasting competitions vary widely in their methodologies, the qualifications of their judges, and fairness. Prestigious international competitions that include all spirit categories are judged by expert tasters, but often only a few have real expertise in tequila. On the other hand, regional tequila-focused competitions tend to be judged by folks who know and love tequila but lack formal training.

In either case, judges taste between a dozen and as many as a hundred samples in a single day. This obviously presents some issues. To stay sober, judges must spit rather than swallow, so no evaluation of the tequila's finish is possible. This is a huge limitation of most competitions. Secondly, even experienced judges can suffer palate fatigue after tasting dozens of samples. Finally, most competitions have no internal controls to ensure that their judges are consistent.

Competitions are best thought of as promotional events. Given tequila's reputation as a "party drink," tasting competitions can help show that it is a beverage to be taken seriously. Images of sober, well-dressed judges sniffing tequila in crystal stemware and taking studious notes are slowly replacing those of spring break binges.

Competitions also have awards. Those taking best in class and gold medals for their tequilas gain bragging rights that can make for valuable marketing; tequilas that do poorly can simply not mention that they competed. Of course, there is little incentive for winners to re-enter competitions they have already won. That is why you see old tequila brands with medals from the nineteenth century on their labels. Once you're at the top, the only way you can go is down.

Competitions give the media and public a reason to talk about tequila. They give winning brands another way to promote themselves. And those medals give new consumers a reason to choose one bottle over another in the store. But more serious tequila aficionados take competition results with a hearty grain of salt. Ultimately, becoming a skilled taster allows you to trust your own mouth more than those of unknown judges.

WHO IS AN EXPERT?

What makes someone a tequila expert, and who decides? The simple truth is that anyone can claim to be a tequila expert, and there is no acknowledged authority that decides who is or isn't an one. Expertise is a funny thing. It mostly depends on a person's ability to claim it with a straight face and to have that claim taken seriously by others. This is certainly true with tequila, where expert status is often claimed by those who have worked in tequila bars, made a single brand-sponsored trip to Jalisco, or completed a one-day course in tequila basics.

A bounty of tequila certification courses has sprung up. For the right price, you can have your pick of self-appointed "authorities" who will certify you as a tequila expert, master taster, or even as a tequila sommelier.

While some of these courses do offer quality education in the basics, others are first and foremost designed to be moneymakers for the people offering them. Any customer who pays the fee will get some kind of certificate. There is no money to be made in flunking people, even if they don't speak the language the class is offered in or understand much of the material.

Be wary of claims to expertise not backed up by years or decades on the ground in Jalisco and of certifiers who claim they can create experts in a few days. The term "tequila sommelier" in particular is a red flag. In wine, sommelier education is intense and conforms to generally understood standards. Trained somms are able to discern subtle nuances and even the origins and vintages of wines in blind tastings. Nothing in the tequila certification world comes remotely close to this kind of training, and trying to apply this French wine term to basic tequila education indicates ignorance at best and cynical disrespect at worst.

HOW TO CHOOSE A TEQUILA

Deciding which tequila to buy can be intimidating. Every state, territory, and province has its own liquor laws and distribution system, so you can't anticipate what the selection might be from one area to the next. Even if you become well versed on the selection and pricing where you live, your local intelligence may be less useful on a business trip or vacation. The following tips will help.

DEFINE YOUR PARAMETERS

Before you set foot in a store, decide what category and class of tequila you are there to buy. This immediately narrows your choices, which will make things easier.

Have a budget in mind. Pricing varies from region to region, but you can get a sense of the local range by looking up prices at a chain liquor store like BevMo or a supermarket (depending on the state).

MIXING OR SIPPING?

There should not be a drastic difference in quality between the tequila you mix and the tequila you sip. Tequila that doesn't taste good neat won't make a cocktail that tastes good either. But most people want to spend less for a mixer than a sipper, and bold flavors that may be too strong when sipped can punch through other ingredients in a well-made cocktail. Stick to your guns: If you sip only 100% agave tequila or typically avoid additives, apply the same standards to your mixing tequila. Pueblo Viejo, Cimarrón, and Espolón are good brands to start with.

WHERE TO BUY?

If you are in a metropolitan area, find a local independent liquor store with a wide selection and knowledgeable staff. They will be more expensive than big chains but will make up for that in customer service. Take tequila seriously enough to ask for help. There is usually at least one tequila fanatic on staff who will be enthusiastic about helping you find an appropriate bottle. Think of them as your "tequila steward." Explain what you're after, what you're willing to spend, and listen to their advice.

If you are in a less urban area, see if you can order tequila online. The retailers in the Resources section (page 240) usually list the states that they cannot deliver to. Most of them feature ratings or reviews of tequilas written by staff or customers, which can be helpful in making a selection. Supplement these with other online reviews, including those of the expert tasting panel on Tequila Matchmaker (see page 190).

KNOW YOUR NOMS

The NOM number on each bottle of tequila (see page 60) is the buyer's best friend. Remember that while there are thousands of tequila brands, there are only around 140 NOM numbers. You should know the NOM of your favorite tequilas as well as the ones you prefer to avoid. When faced with an unknown brand of the category and class you're looking for, the first thing you should check is the NOM number. This will often give you a quick yea or nay.

WHAT NOT TO USE: PRICE AND LABEL

Remember that the category, class, and NOM number on a tequila label are regulated by law, but most of the label is just branding. Know the category and class of tequila you want, have some opinions about a few NOM numbers, and stick to a reasonable budget. The brand name and label aesthetics should not matter unless you're looking to make a particular impression with a gift. Price matters, but only to a point. Anything that costs less than $20 should raise suspicions about ingredient quality and ethics. On the other hand, many expensive tequilas are simply there to part fools and their money. Don't be a fool: Develop a sense for what quality tequila costs, and be skeptical of overpriced outliers.

THE RISE OF NON-MEXICAN TEQUILA-STYLE SPIRITS

Despite some legitimate criticism, the DOT has been undeniably successful in protecting the "tequila" name globally, and it has drastically reduced the number of fake tequilas on the market. Before the Mexican government negotiated crackdowns in the 1970s, pseudo-tequilas were widespread. Since the creation of the CRT in 1994 and the later enforcement of Geographical Indications by the World Trade Organization, Mexico's monopoly on legitimate tequila has been enforced in nearly every country in the world.

But no one can be prevented from growing agave and distilling it into a "tequila-style" spirit. In 2020, the US government recognized "agave spirits" made anywhere in the world as an official category. Entrepreneurs in a handful of countries are already producing tequila-style agave spirits. The expansion of tequila-style spirits into the global market can be controversial, but without a doubt it will greatly increase in the coming decades.

As of 2023, there were around thirty growers in California and seven distilleries making "California agave spirit," which by state law must be made from 100% California-grown agave, free of any additives. A handful of distillers in Australia and South Africa are making agave spirits in both tequila and mezcal styles. All three areas have the right climate for growing agave. All three have world-class wine industries and the fermentation know-how and supply chains that come with that. And all three are regional economic powerhouses with access to densely populated markets. While Australia and California have much higher labor costs than Mexico does, their other comparative advantages could lead to success down the line.

Opposite page: Agave farming in Australia, and the crest of the California Agave Council.

Criticism of these projects ranges from the ethical to the practical. Many in Mexico decry the creation of in-all-but-name tequilas in countries where the agave isn't native and a distilling tradition has been imported rather than inherited. Some see it simply as unfair competition for real tequila, but others go so far as to call it cultural appropriation. Milder criticism emphasizes the difference in production costs between Mexico—with low wages and widespread knowledge of tequila production—and developed countries with high wages and little direct experience in the idiosyncrasies of turning agave into palatable liquor. Indeed, in the short term, agave spirits produced in these three countries cannot hope to compete with real tequila in price.

Nevertheless, cultivation of drought-resistant agave in California and Australia expands yearly, and brands that are equal parts investment and hobby put faith in aficionados' seemingly endless thirst for the innovative, the novel, and the collectible.

TEQUILA COCKTAILS

Tequila was not well known in the United States during the late nineteenth and early twentieth centuries, when cocktails were being created. Few cocktail chroniclers include tequila drinks among the classics. But in the late twentieth century, both the margarita and the tequila sunrise became massively popular and fueled North American demand for tequila. While the sunrise fad came and went, the margarita has become a staple of cocktail culture, and many consider it to be the most popular cocktail in the United States. The craft cocktail movement of the early 2000s enthusiastically embraced tequila as a base spirit for innovative new concoctions, as well as a novel substitute for vodka, gin, and whiskey in many classic drinks.

In Mexico, craft cocktails are still a niche phenomenon priced well beyond the budget of the average drinker. Tequila is commonly mixed with soft drinks or soda water, however. Whether at family gatherings or in clubs, the most common way to drink tequila in Mexico is at a shared table with a bottle, a bucket of ice, and various soft drinks that people use to mix to their own taste. Mexicans consume an enormous amount of soft drinks, and the paloma and batanga are two of the most popular tequila cocktails in Mexico.

Good tequila and quality ingredients will make better cocktails. Real fruit juice is a must, and lowballing the quality of triple sec or grenadine can turn an otherwise tasty drink into a syrupy disaster.

....

Cocktail recipes courtesy of Andrés Morán Gutiérrez.

PALOMA | MARGARITA
BATANGA | TEQUILA SUNRISE

PALOMA

If Mexico were to have an official tequila cocktail, the paloma would be it. Blanco tequila and grapefruit just work well together. It's difficult to go wrong with even a hastily prepared tequila and Squirt on ice, although using quality ingredients raises this cocktail to the level of the sublime. Some fancier recipes use fresh grapefruit juice, which can be great, but it will add a bitterness that makes grapefruit soda, simple syrup, or some variety of sweetener necessary for a well-balanced drink.

Rock salt

Ice

1½ ounces (45 ml) 100% agave tequila blanco

¾ ounce (20 ml) lime juice

Grapefruit soda, ideally Squirt (approximately 1 to 1¼ ounces / 30 to 40 ml)

Grapefruit slice, for garnish

Rim a chimney glass with rock salt and fill it with ice. Add the tequila and lime juice, and top with grapefruit soda. Stir until the glass is ice cold. Garnish with a grapefruit slice.

MARGARITA

These days, a wide gamut of drinks is served under the name margarita. There are almost as many competing stories about the drink's origin, although most of them place it relatively close to the Mexico-US border. Debates over the cocktail's provenance become less interesting, however, when you know that *margarita* is Spanish for "daisy," and that daisy is the name of a family of classic cocktails made from a base spirit, citrus, and a sweetener. So the margarita is simply a tequila daisy, and it was probably created independently by any number of bilingual bartenders who were working with tequila in the early- to mid-twentieth century.

Like the daisy, there are myriad variations on the margarita, especially regarding proportions and the sweetener used. As with any cocktail, your mileage may vary depending on the quality of ingredients used. Experiment with different tequilas, triple secs, and types of lime until you find your perfect margarita.

Rock salt (optional)

Ice

1½ ounces (45 ml) 100% agave tequila blanco

1 ounce (30 ml) triple sec

1 ounce (30 ml) lime juice

Lime slice, for garnish

If you like a salty margarita, rim a cocktail glass with salt. In a shaker, combine the tequila, triple sec, lime juice, and ice. Shake until it is ice cold, and strain into the glass. Garnish with a slice of lime.

BATANGA · CHARRO NEGRO

The *charro negro* ("black cowboy") is as ubiquitous as the paloma. In Mexico, epic amounts of Coca-Cola are consumed, and the combination of tequila, Coke, and lime is perhaps the most common way of drinking tequila in the whole country.

The batanga is a version of the charro negro served as the house cocktail at Cantina La Capilla in the town of Tequila. Its creator, the late, beloved Don Javier Delgado Corona, named the drink after an old friend. The batanga is distinguished from other charros negros in the fine details: It is always served in a chimney glass; it is rimmed with coarse rock salt; and it is stirred with the knife used to cut the lime, in honor of Don Javier. The original recipe called for a "generous portion" of tequila, and it is served with about 3 ounces at La Capilla. The version here privileges balance over firepower.

Rock salt

Ice

1½ ounces (45 ml) 100% agave tequila blanco

½ ounce (15 ml) lime juice (about one juicy Key lime)

Top with cola, ideally Mexican Coca-Cola (approximately 1½ to 1¾ ounces / 45 to 55 ml)

Lime wedge, for garnish

Rim a chimney glass with rock salt and fill with ice. Add the tequila and lime juice. Top the glass with the cola and stir with a long knife until the glass is ice cold, Don Javier style. Garnish with a lime wedge.

TEQUILA SUNRISE

You don't see sunrises on many cocktail menus these days, but this sweet drink played a monumental role in tequila's popularization in the 1970s. Perhaps surprisingly, this was thanks to the Rolling Stones.

An updated version of the 1930s classic (which replaced crème de cassis with grenadine) was served to the Stones in California early in their 1972 Exile on Main Street tour. The band loved the drink so much that they required concert venues to supply the ingredients backstage and consumed an astonishing number of sunrises on the rest of the tour.

Ice

1¼ ounces (50 ml) 100% agave tequila blanco

2 ounces (60 ml) orange juice

½ ounce (15 ml) grenadine

Orange slice, for garnish

Cherry, for garnish

Fill a tall glass with ice. Add the tequila and the orange juice to the glass. Slowly add the grenadine and allow it to sink to the bottom. Garnish with an orange slice and cherry.

READY-TO-DRINK TEQUILA COCKTAILS

"Beverages containing tequila" were recognized by the 2012 tequila Norm, and these products are regulated to ensure that the tequila used in them is legitimate and that they have been blended and packaged under the purview of the CRT. In the late 2000s and 2010s, ready-to-drink canned and bottled beverages (RTDs) began reshaping the alcoholic beverage industry worldwide. In the United States, most RTDs are malt-based, but premade cocktails with a liquor base are gobbling up a growing share of the category. Among them, tequila is the second-most popular base spirit. In 2020, Tequila Herradura's New Mix line was the third-best-selling RTD worldwide, making it the tequila maker's top-selling product.

In the United States, tequila has always been consumed primarily in cocktails, and RTDs are ideal for those who are too inexperienced, intimidated, or short on time to make their own cocktails at home. This convenience seems likely to ensure their continued growth in the coming decades.

VISITING TEQUILA COUNTRY

A visit to "Tequila Country" is the only way to directly experience tequila production. Seeing, smelling, and tasting at different steps in the production process will hone your palate unlike anything else. And speaking with jimadores, distillers, and other locals will enhance your appreciation for the human element behind the drink. Thanks to an expanding tourism and service sector, it's never been easier to visit the region.

When planning a trip to Tequila Country, the first question is whether you will organize it yourself or hire a guide or tour company. For most travelers, hiring a tour professional is well worth the cost and can result in an experience that you simply could not arrange on your own. For one thing, few tequila distilleries offer public tours. Tequila Country is very different from most of the world's wine regions in that you can't simply arrive at the front gate of most distilleries and expect anything but confused looks and polite rejection. A reputable guide will have access to many places that you don't. However, some travelers with particular skills and dispositions will prefer to go it alone.

Next, you'll need to decide whether to base yourself in Guadalajara or stay in one or more of the small producing towns. Guadalajara is a city of several million people and offers a plethora of lodging and dining options for every budget. It is only an hour east of Tequila and two hours west of Los Altos, so

Most of Tequila's principal attractions are within walking distance of the town center.

it makes a convenient base for visiting both regions without changing hotels. Tequila is the only town in the Valley with good options for lodging. The few hotels in the Highlands tend toward the basic.

GOING SOLO?

It's easy to book your own tours at a handful of Valley distilleries, and a few of them don't even require reservations (see Resources, page 240). To organize your own tequila trip, you need to be able to speak Spanish well enough to communicate over the phone with distilleries and service providers. While it's easier than ever to reach tequila distilleries via email and social media, phoning is still the quickest, most reliable way to make plans in Jalisco.

As you plan your itinerary, avoid the temptation to cram too much into any one day. Having to cut short someone's hospitality to dash off to your next visit feels terrible and will leave a bad impression with your hosts. Two distilleries per day is the absolute maximum. For most people, one is plenty. Remember that in addition to touring the distillery, tasting the tequila, and socializing with your hosts, you must allow

time for meals between visits, traffic between destinations, and the inevitable delays of traveling in Mexico.

HIRING A GUIDE

Qualified, professional tour operators have relationships with smaller and less touristy distilleries and can provide this access to you for a price. The best will also handle ground transportation, meals, and even lodging. Every year, however, the tequila tour market grows, and some of the new entrants are unqualified, unscrupulous, and uninsured, and they may even attempt to copy the names and business models of more reliable providers.

When vetting a tour provider, the two most important questions to ask are how much experience they have and what kind of insurance they carry. Online reviewing platforms like TripAdvisor can be used to verify a provider's experience and the general level of client satisfaction. Be sure that your tour provider's insurance will cover anything not covered by your own travel insurance policy.

Next, you should ask the guide or company about their educational background in the tequila industry as well as what distilleries you'll visit. If you're not careful, you may think you're booking with an expert and arrive to find that your actual guide is a well-meaning teenager with no formal training or experience in the tequila industry. That type of tour can be enjoyable if all you're after is a buzz and some photo ops. But the tours with high staff turnover that specialize in multiple, quick stops to distilleries along the highway are a world away from boutique operators who offer educational experiences based on personal relationships within the industry.

Unforeseen things happen, and no guide can guarantee what distilleries you will visit, but they should tell you which distilleries they plan to take you to as well as what the backup destinations will be if those plans fall through.

Opposite page: Distillery tours can be booked well in advance, or at the last minute on Tequila's main street, Sixto Gorjón.

TRAVEL ADVICE

Traveling in the tequila region is different from visiting Mexican coastal towns and resorts. This is arguably "the real Mexico," and consequently, far less English is spoken and so a bit more planning and forethought is required.

TEQUILA TRAVEL BASICS

Guadalajara's Miguel Hidalgo y Costilla International Airport (GDL) is about an hour and a half from Tequila, if traffic is light. It takes at least four hours to drive to Tequila from Puerto Vallarta, so a day trip isn't feasible.

If you intend to add to your tequila collection while in Mexico, plan accordingly. Mexico places no limit on how much tequila you take out of the country, although most airlines' official limit is five liters per person. Most countries and US states have policies on bringing in, declaring, and paying duties on liquor, and it is your responsibility to know them. Failure to declare your liquid treasure can lead to serious penalties. In the United States, the duty assessed on declared liquor is nominal.

WEATHER AND TIME OF YEAR

Historically, Jalisco's rainy season runs from June through early September, and the summer months are hot as well. While the afternoon thunderstorms are breathtaking, experienced travelers avoid the warm, muggy summer months, when many of the smaller distilleries also slow down or stop production. May is typically dry, but it is also the hottest month of the year. It's also peak wildfire season, so there is often smoke in the air.

The weather in Jalisco from late September through April is warm and mostly dry, and January through March is the ideal time to escape the northern US and Canadian winter.

Holy Week (the week before Easter) is best avoided, as most of the distilleries will be closed. The same goes for the Christmas holidays, which in Mexico begin on December 12, the Day of the Virgin of

Guadalupe, and continue until January 6, the Day of the Three Kings. Tequila's town festival is usually held during the first two weeks of December. It's less likely that you will see active tequila production at smaller distilleries during these holidays.

These days, tequila production and agave harvesting are essentially year-round activities, although both endeavors may slow down during the summer rainy season. If you hope to catch agave being planted, sometime between March and May is your best bet.

GETTING AROUND

If you're planning to drink or you're inexperienced at driving in Mexican cities, do yourself a favor and leave transportation to the pros. Private transportation is a booming business in Guadalajara, and a web search will yield myriad options.

If you're in a hurry to get to Tequila and don't want to make stops along the way, take an official airport cab from GDL. There are ticket booths inside the terminal, and a fare to Tequila costs around US$100. Be sure your driver knows that you want to take the faster toll road (*autopista* or *cuota*), and you should also make sure that the toll is included in the fare.

If you're in Guadalajara, you can hire a taxi for a day trip to the Valley or to take you to your hotel in Tequila—with or without stops at distilleries on your route. This can be an affordable way to have a private driver and chat with someone who likely knows the region well. Be sure to negotiate a price up front and be clear about how long you will need the driver so that you will be able to make the stops you want and so on. Generally, if you're hiring a *taxista* for several hours or the whole day, they will be happy to make all the stops you like. Guadalajara taxis aren't very large or comfortable, and be aware that passenger seat belts are uncommon. You may be able to convince drivers of rideshare services to take you to Tequila, but they're unlikely to make stops and usually need to get permission before proceeding. If you choose this option, keep in mind that the driver will have a long "deadhead" trip with no passengers on the way back to the city, and tip accordingly.

If your budget is very limited, you can take a local bus from the old Guadalajara bus station, La Antigua Central, or from the bus station on the outskirts of Zapopan—note that these buses do not leave from the new station in Tonalá. They make frequent stops and keep a fairly loose schedule. But they are a great way to absorb a lot of local flavor and will drop you off near the center of Tequila.

If you decide to rent a car and drive yourself, be sure you understand the rental contract—it's a good idea to book online and in English. Your foreign car insurance is not valid in Mexico, and it's recommended to either purchase full coverage or use a credit card that provides full

coverage. Take the toll road rather than the free highway to Tequila. Do not drink and drive! In addition to the other serious and obvious reasons not to drink and drive, getting a DWI will nullify rental insurance and is an excellent way to end up in jail.

SAFETY

Traffic and automobiles are by far the most dangerous things you are likely to encounter on your trip to Mexico. Roads may not be well maintained, driver training is minimal, the rules of the road are different (and may appear to be nonexistent). Sadly, driving under the influence is common around Tequila, especially on the weekends. In the event of an accident, medical assistance may be slow to arrive, and the care given may leave something to be desired.

For all these reasons, it is strongly recommended that you not drive yourself, unless you have experience driving in the region and have absolutely no plans to drink.

Pedestrians should exercise the usual degree of caution in small tequila-producing towns where drivers are considerate but increasingly frustrated by tourists who walk out into traffic. More caution should be taken in Guadalajara, where driving is aggressive and the pedestrian right-of-way is not keenly observed.

You will probably see police everywhere you go. They will probably be doing things the police where you live don't do (e.g., using their flashing lights when there isn't an emergency, traveling in large groups, carrying long guns, etc.). This can be alarming at first, but it doesn't mean there is anything to worry about. You are unlikely to have any direct interaction with the police.

Carrying an alcoholic beverage in an open container in the wrong context is also a good way to end up in trouble. You will see tourists sauntering around with drinks in Tequila, and while it is tolerated by the police, it is frowned upon by locals. You should absolutely not do this in Guadalajara or in the Highlands.

Opposite page: The late Don Javier Delgado Corona, founder of the historic Cantina La Capilla, exemplified Tequila's spirit of hospitality.

TEQUILA TRAVEL SPANISH

Hiring a guide means not having to worry about issues of language and interpretation. If you go it alone, most distilleries will have someone who speaks enough English to show you around. But in dealing with everyday people, including restaurant staff, knowing some basic Spanish will go a long way toward making a good impression and avoiding misunderstandings. Here are some basic words you'll find useful when traveling in Tequila Country.

PLACES	
(Agave) field	Campo (de agave)
ATM	Cajero (automático)
Bar	Bar
Distillery	Destilería
Liquor store	Licorería
Store	Tienda
TEQUILA PROCESS	
Additives	Abocantes/aditivos
Aging	Añejamiento
Barrel	Barrica
Bottling	Envasado
Cooking	Cocción
Copper	Cobre
(Double) Distillation	(Doble) destilación
Extraction	Extracción
Fermentation	Fermentación
Harvest	Cosecha
(Roller) Mill	Molino
Oak	Roble
Oven	Horno
Planting	Siembra
(Stainless) Steel	Acero (inoxidable)
Still	Alambique
Tank (for fermentation)	Tina (de fermentación)

FAQS	
How do I get to . . . ?	¿Cómo llego a . . . ?
Are there tours?	¿Hay tours?
Is it 100% agave?	¿Es cien-por-ciento de agave?
What class of tequila is this?	¿Qué clase de tequila es?
Can you show me the bottle, please?	¿Me enseña la botella, por favor?
How much does it cost for a glass/for a bottle?	¿Cuánto cuesta por copa/por botella?
How long was it barrel aged?	¿Cuánto tiempo llevó en barrica?
What is its ABV?	¿Cuántos grados alcóholicos tiene?

TEQUILA TASTING AND DRINKING	
It tastes (like) . . .	Sabe (a) . . .
Astringent	Astringente
Bitter	Amargo
Citric	Cítrico
Cocktail	Coctel
Cooked	Cocido
Dry	Seco
Earthy	Terroso
Finish	Retrogusto
Fruity	Frutal
Glass (for tasting)	Copa
Glass (shot)	Caballito
Herbal	Herbal
Ice	Hielo
Mineral	Mineral
Neat/straight	Derecho
On the rocks	En las rocas
Raw	Crudo
Sip	Traguito
Smooth	Suave
Sour	Ácido
Spices	Especias
Spicy	Picante
Sweet	Dulce
Tasty	Rico

AFTERWORD
Sustaining Tequila

Tequila has some problems. The problems of tequila are the problems of the world: A narrow focus on economic growth at all costs threatens ecological balance, climate change disrupts previously reliable conditions, and the gap between economic insiders and outsiders grows wider every year. Tequila's very success has created conditions that may be difficult to sustain. How these challenges are confronted will determine whether the industry can survive as it now exists for even another fifty or a hundred years.

A FLAWED GEOGRAPHICAL INDICATION

Critics see some issues plaguing tequila as the result of an inherently flawed Geographical Indication: Tequila's Denomination of Origin. GIs are supposed to improve rural communities' economic well-being while protecting traditional knowledge and the environment. Studies have found that the DOT has done the opposite: It has channeled profit away from tequila-producing communities and into the pockets of large corporations, encouraged the adoption of industrial techniques over traditional ones, and caused ecological harm. In the academic literature, the DOT is seen as an example of a GI that has failed those it is meant to benefit.

While tequila is now a multi-billion-dollar industry, its massive profits haven't resulted in widespread socioeconomic benefits. In the Tequila Valley, poverty and modest educational achievement persist in the shadow of enormous wealth.

Traditional agave cultivation methods have been largely replaced by chemical-intensive agronomy, and complex reverse-leasing arrangements empower large tequila makers at the expense of small agave farmers. Some of the most traditional tequileros have either opted out of the DOT or were never included in the first place. These producers find other ways to make a living, but the tequila category is diminished by their absence. For most tequileros, traditional tequila production is possible only as a sideline to other, more reliable sources of income. In this sense, the DOT has failed in one of its primary tasks: making traditional tequila production a viable livelihood for all the families who have kept the tradition alive.

BLUE AGAVE MONOCULTURE

Tequila's exclusive use of the blue agave and reliance on cloning have produced a dangerous monoculture. The blue agave became favored for tequila production in part because it produces many clones (hijuelos), which become mature plants much faster than seeds do. But this monoculture means that the entire tequila industry is just one infestation or extreme weather event away from agroindustrial collapse.

Planting clones ensures that the strengths of the parent plant are passed to the next generation, but weaknesses are also passed down. So while the blue agave's genetics remain frozen in time, its natural enemies continue to evolve. The most successful pests will thrive and pass along their genes. Predators become ever-more adept at destroying agaves, and each generation of agaves becomes more helpless.

Lack of genetic diversity also prevents the blue agave from responding to the evolutionary pressure of climate change. If agaves were reproducing sexually, those best able to withstand extreme weather would survive to pass along their genes and less resilient lines would die off. But just as with pests, the entire blue agave population is equally vulnerable to extreme temperatures due to monoculture.

A single freeze, drought, or blight might be all it takes to end tequila as we know it, and there have been some close calls already. In the late nineteenth century, blue agave was planted in Los Altos for the first time after a fungus decimated the Tequila Valley agave crop. Los Altos suffered massive agave losses in 1997 when the first freeze in a hundred years hit the region. Since that "once-a-century" event, there have been two more freezes in Los Altos.

Scientists have been sounding alarms about the potential consequences of agave monocropping since the 1990s, but industry leaders have insisted that the solutions proposed by botanists and ecologists are impossible (or too expensive) to implement.

One strategy is to allow some percentage of agaves to flower and produce seeds. A handful of producers have begun doing this. The nascent Bat Friendly Project (see page 34) is another effort in this direction.

The main obstacle to this strategy is that it cuts into the profit margin of agave growers and, in the short term, reduces tequila production. No one wants to be the only grower to lose money for the long-term benefit of the greater industry. This is a situation where the market incentive of short-term gain is at odds with the ultimate survival of tequila itself.

Increasing the agave's genetic diversity through a program of cross-breeding would require resources, planning, cooperation, and careful execution. It would take a decade to produce the first generation of plants. Advocates of this plan argue that there is no time to lose, while cynics maintain that it is already too late and that the tequila industry is too riven with conflict to enact such a plan.

Another possible solution to the monoculture problem is even more controversial because it would require changing the definition of tequila itself. For most of its history, tequila was made with a handful of sub-varietals of what's now called *Agave tequilana*. While the blue agave became the preferred sub-varietal used to make tequila in the late nineteenth century, the others weren't excluded until 1964. Softening this hard line against other varietals that had been previously used to make tequila is another possible way to reverse some of the damage of monoculture.

Industry leaders become apoplectic when this is suggested, arguing that allowing other agaves into tequila would pollute the genetic purity of the blue agave, reduce efficiencies, and essentially be the end of tequila as we know it—which, in a way, is precisely the point. Ecologists warn that tequila as we know it is built on a shaky foundation of monocultural susceptibility to pests and extreme weather.

Hidden away in remote canyons and on hillsides, the blue agave's cousins in the wild have been evolving defenses to these threats. It's possible they could help save the day. After all, other, closely related *tequilana* varietals (see page 30) were part of tequila's historical flavor profile. The very fact that they may be able to cross-breed with blue agave shows that they are not radically distinct and that the lines drawn between sub-varietals are somewhat arbitrary and easily transcended in nature. The prohibition against using non-blue *Agave tequilana* to make tequila was not brought down from some mountaintop on stone tablets. It was an economic decision that could be undone just as easily. Resistance to doing so may be the downfall of tequila itself.

ENVIRONMENTAL DEGRADATION

Like any industry, tequila impacts the natural environment. Its effects include deforestation, the overapplication of chemical fertilizers and pesticides, and the liquid waste produced as a by-product of production.

By the 1870s, observers were already commenting on deforestation in the Tequila Valley. Native trees were felled in ever greater numbers to feed the boilers running the booming industry's ovens and stills and to make room for sun-seeking agave.

Tequila's industrial growth sputtered during the chaotic first half of the twentieth century, when petroleum products also replaced timber as a fuel source. After the end of the Mexican Revolution in 1921, farmers tended to plant agave as a kind of insurance crop on marginal land where nothing else would grow. Agave was a nest egg they hoped would pay off years down the line, while they survived on staple food crops.

But free trade agreements have made it cheaper to buy imported food than to grow it locally. Add high agave prices to this scenario, and it is no surprise that struggling farmers clear land and plant more agave at the expense of traditional subsistence crops like corn and beans.

During the historic agave price surge that began in the late 2000s and has continued into the early 2020s, entire hillsides were clear-cut (legally and otherwise) to make room for agave. This deforestation contributes to global warming, drives out local fauna, diminishes air quality, and sets the stage for the erosion of precious soil nutrients.

Even farmers who have inherited traditional agave cultivation knowledge have strong financial incentives to turn to more industrial, chemically intensive methods to extract higher yields in less time. Amateur agave farmers are even more vulnerable to these pressures. Lured by the promise of "blue gold," hundreds of inexperienced growers got into the business in the years around 2020. Many quickly discovered that young agave plants struggle where the soil composition and pH are inappropriate. Agricultural supply companies swooped in, aggressively selling a regimen of fertilizers, soil sealants, pesticides, herbicides, and fungicides as blanket cure-alls for whatever ails the agave. Few of these novice farmers have the resources or patience to consult traditional agaveros or professional agronomists who might more precisely diagnose and treat the problems in their fields. Chemicals accumulate in the soil, in groundwater, and possibly in the bodies of the workers who apply them and live nearby.

Compounding the potential environmental damage, tequila production necessarily creates large amounts of vinazas, or stillage: liquid waste that must be treated before being released. If untreated, vinazas' temperature, pH, and oxygen demand can make surface water deadly to life-forms ranging from microbes to fish. More than ten liters of vinazas are produced for every liter of tequila, meaning more than 5 billion liters of liquid waste were released into the environment in 2021 alone. Mexican law requires vinazas to be treated before release, which is a simple but expensive process. Enforcement of these laws is haphazard, and the release of untreated waste into streams and rivers is common.

The cumulative effects of monoculture-driven deforestation, chemical-intensive farming, and liquid waste are significant challenges for the tequila industry. To date, there is no coordinated plan to address these problems, which have grown right along with the industry. Locals, especially those who are not cashing in on the agave boom, feel helpless in the face of the dramatic remaking of the landscape where they grew up, while Mexican scientists insist that to be more green, Jalisco may need to become less blue.

REASONS FOR HOPE

Despite these immense challenges, there are reasons to keep hope alive. Many tequileros are cognizant of these issues and are making the changes necessary to confront them. To do so without going bust, they need educated consumers who ask brands hard questions and are prepared to pay a bit more to support sustainable tequila.

Tequila aficionados tend to be kind, caring people who truly appreciate Mexico and the communities that have kept the tequila tradition alive for centuries. They see the effects of ecological harm and economic injustice all around them and are actively seeking ways to mitigate these harms through their purchasing choices.

Beyond supporting the tequila brands that do the right thing, aficionados are also increasingly active in support of the scholars, activists, and nonprofits who are advocating for policy changes in Mexico that seek balance and justice in the tequila industry (see Resources, page 240). For tequila-producing communities to thrive, solidarity will be necessary.

GLOSSARY

100% AGAVE TEQUILA Tequila whose sole sugar source is the blue agave.

ABOCANTES Additives intended to smooth or soften a tequila's flavor. The Norm permits the use of caramel color, natural oak extract, glycerin, and sugar-based syrups as abocantes. A tequila containing abocantes may be called *abocado*, although this designation is not required by the Norm.

ABV Alcohol by volume. The percentage of ethyl alcohol in a beverage. Tequila may have an ABV ranging from 35% to 55%.

ADDITIVE Generic term for sweeteners, colorants, aromas, and flavorings added to otherwise finished tequila to impart or intensify its color, aroma, or taste. The Norm allows any additive permitted by Mexico's Secretariat of Health to be used.

AGAVE A genus of succulent plants native to the American continent. Also called "maguey" or "mezcal" in different parts of Mexico, and "century plant" in the United States.

AGAVE TEQUILANA **WEBER, BLUE VARIETY** Sub-species of agave that must be used in tequila production. Commonly called "blue agave."

AGUAMIEL Diluted, cooked agave juice that results from extraction. In pulque-producing regions, refers to raw agave sap.

ALCOHOLS Organic chemical compounds containing an -OH group. In tequila, ethanol, methanol, and superior alcohols are all regulated by the Norm.

ALDEHYDES Organic chemical compounds containing a -CHO group, formed by the oxidation of primary alcohols. In tequila, aldehydes contribute aroma and are regulated by the Norm.

ALEMBIC Pot still. Also used to describe the distillation process that uses such a still. See *pot distillation*.

AÑEJO TEQUILA Tequila aged at least one year in oak barrels of no more than 600 liters.

AGAVE

AUTOCLAVE Stainless-steel pressure cooker used to hydrolyze agave.

BAGAZO Leftover agave fiber from which aguamiel has been extracted. In some rural dialects, the initial consonants are transposed, and the word is *gabazo*.

BATIDOR Historically, the worker who entered the fermentation tanks and separated agave fiber to begin the fermentation process. Also called a *revolvedor*.

BLANCO TEQUILA Tequila with no more than sixty days of contact with oak.

BLUE AGAVE Common name for *Agave tequilana* Weber, blue variety. The only agave sub-species permitted in tequila production.

CABALLITO "Little horse." A tall, thin Mexican shot glass that evolved from the *cuernito*. While not appropriate for serious tasting, it is a staple of cantina drinking.

CAPAR "To castrate." To sever the quiote from the agave. An agave whose quiote has been removed is described as *capado*.

CNIT Cámara Nacional de la Industria Tequilera (National Chamber of the Tequila Industry). An industry association formed in 1959 as the Regional Chamber of the Tequila Industry. The CNIT advocates for its members within the CRT and beyond.

BAGAZO

COA DE JIMA Circular bladed tool used by the jimador to harvest blue agave.

COA DE LIMPIEZA Triangular bladed tool used to weed agave fields.

COGOLLO Cluster of new, tender pencas sprouting from the top of a growing agave. Often removed before cooking the agave because its high wax content may impart bitterness.

COLUMN DISTILLATION Distillation process in which vapor rises through a column containing various metal plates, resulting in multiple distillations in a single pass. The process can be operated without shutting down between batches and can result in a much higher alcohol yield. Also called "continuous distillation."

CONGENER In tequila, the generic term for minor chemical compounds that impart aroma and flavor. The most important classes of congeners are superior alcohols, esters, and aldehydes.

CONTINUOUS DISTILLATION See *column distillation.*

CONTRACT BRAND A brand owned by an entity other than the tequila maker. Also called a *maquila.*

CRT Consejo Regulador del Tequila (Tequila Regulatory Council). Nongovernmental organization authorized by the Mexican government to monitor tequila production, enforce the tequila Norm, certify tequilas, and promote the category worldwide.

CUERNITO "Little horn." A real cow horn traditionally used to drink tequila.

CUT In distillation, to start collecting the body of a distillate after the heads have passed or to stop collecting the body, diverting the tails to another container.

DAMAJUANA "Demijohn," literally "Lady Jane." A large, narrow-necked bottle used to transport tequila before the advent of mass-produced glass bottles and steel tankers.

DESTROZAMIENTO "Destroying." In tequila production, refers to the first distillation in a pot still.

DIFFUSER Machine used to extract raw agave juice for subsequent hydrolysis. Can also be used to extract aguamiel from cooked agave.

DISCONTINUOUS DISTILLATION See *pot distillation.*

DISTILLATION The process of purifying a liquid by successive evaporation and condensation. In the case of tequila, its primary purpose is to remove water and concentrate ethyl alcohol.

DO *Denominación de origen* (Denomination of Origin). The Mexican system of GIs. The Denomination of Origin for Tequila (DOT) defines tequila's production region as anywhere in the state of Jalisco and in certain municipalities of the states of Guanajuato, Michoacán, Nayarit, and Tamaulipas.

ESTERS Organic chemical compounds formed by interaction between an alcohol and an acid. Esters contribute many aromas and flavors to tequila.

ETHANOL "Beverage alcohol." Its chemical formula is C_2H_5OH.

EXTRA-AÑEJO TEQUILA Tequila aged at least three years in oak barrels of no more than 600 liters.

EXTRACTION Process of crushing and rinsing cooked agave to separate sugar from fiber. Or, in a diffuser process, leaching out of carbohydrates from raw agave fiber.

FERMENTATION Biochemical process in which microbes convert a carbohydrate into an alcohol or an acid. In tequila, the primary type of fermentation is yeast converting sugars to ethanol.

FLIGHT Tasting of selected tequilas, organized in a specific sequence.

FORMULATION Process of preparing aguamiel for fermentation. May involve dilution, the addition of mieles dulces, other sugars, and/or yeast.

FURFURAL Organic chemical compound regulated by the Norm. Gives aromas of toasted nuts and seeds, including coffee.

GI Geographical Indication. The generic term for the protected status enjoyed by products that by law can be produced only in a specific area. Mexico's GIs are known as Denominations of Origin (DOs).

GOLD TEQUILA Also called *oro* or *joven*. Usually a mixto containing caramel color and flavorings. All 100% agave golds are a blend of blanco and one or more other classes of tequila.

HEADS Liquid condensed and collected at the beginning of distillation before the first cut has been made.

HIGHLANDS see *Los Altos*.

HIJUELOS Vegetative clones produced by blue agaves.

HORNO "Oven." Refers to the stone ovens used by many producers to cook agave.

JIMA Agave harvest.

JIMADOR Skilled farmworker who harvests agave.

LOS ALTOS Highland region of Jalisco east of Guadalajara, bordering the states of Guanajuato, Aguascalientes, Zacatecas, and Michoacán. The primary tequila-producing towns of the Highlands are Arandas, Tepatitlán, Atotonilco el Alto, and Jesús María.

MAGUEY Another name for agave in Mexico, brought by the Spanish from the Caribbean. In contemporary Jalisco, often used to refer to non-*tequilana* agaves used to make pulque or mezcal.

MESOAMERICA Roughly, present-day Mexico and Central America.

METHANOL Alcohol regulated by the Norm whose chemical formula is CH_3OH.

MEZCAL In most of Mexico, a traditional agave distillate. Since 1997, mezcal has its own DO limiting its production to certain states. In Jalisco, "mezcal" is a traditional word for "agave," especially those used to make spirits.

MIELES AMARGAS "Bitter honeys." Dirty water that runs off agaves during the first few hours of cooking in ovens and autoclaves. It is generally extracted and discarded with the vinazas.

JIMADOR

PENCA

MIELES DULCES "Sweet honeys." Cooked agave syrup that is extracted from ovens and autoclaves. It can be used to raise the sugar content of aguamiel during formulation or to start fermentation.

MIXTO "Mixed." Refers to the sugar source of any non-100% agave tequila. The term is not recognized by the CRT and does not appear in the Norm or on tequila labels.

MOSTO MUERTO "Dead must." The "agave beer" resulting from fermentation of aguamiel. The liquid that will be distilled into ordinario or tequila.

MOSTO VIVO "Living must." Actively fermenting aguamiel.

NOM Norma Oficial Mexicana (Official Mexican Norm). Various NOMs set out regulations for different sectors of the Mexican economy. What is usually referred to as "the" NOM (or Norm) in the context of tequila is NOM—006-SCFI-2012, Bebidas alcohólicas—Tequila—Especificaciones.

NORM See *NOM.*

NOVILLO Agave that is mature but has not produced a quiote.

ORDINARIO "Ordinary." Liquid resulting from the first pot distillation of mosto muerto. Usually 20% to 25% ABV.

ORGANOLEPTIC Having qualities that can be perceived sensorily.

PENCA Spiky leaf of the agave.

PIÑA "Pineapple." Common name for the agave stem that is harvested for tequila production. Also called *bola* (ball), *cabeza* (head), or *corazón* (heart).

PIPÓN A large wooden vat used to rest or blend tequila.

POSTURE Discrete period of time tequila spends in a barrel. Every posture wears the barrel down a bit.

POT DISTILLATION Also called "alembic," "Arabic," or "discontinuous distillation." Distillation in which an alcoholic liquid starts in the "pot" at the base of the still, where it is heated. The process must be stopped and restarted for each batch of mosto muerto or ordinario in tequila.

PREMIUM Used as a marketing term with no regulated definition. The Distilled Spirits Council of the US uses "premium" as a price category. In 2022, premium tequilas were those retailing for around $25 to $30 per 750 ml bottle in retail stores.

PULQUE Fermented alcoholic beverage made from the raw sap of various non-*tequilana* agave species.

PURO "Pure." Sometimes used in relation to 100% agave tequila, referring to its sugar source.

QUIOTE The inflorescence (flower stalk) that some agaves grow upon reaching maturity.

RAICILLA Traditional agave distillate from western Jalisco. A DO for raicilla was declared in 2019.

REPOSADO TEQUILA Tequila "rested" in oak for at least two months.

ROLLER MILL Machine most commonly used for extraction. A modified sugar cane mill.

SACCHAROMYCES CEREVISIAE The species of yeast most commonly used in tequila production.

SANGRITA "Little blood." Traditional Jaliscan accompaniment to tequila, made in dozens of different ways, but always with a base of acidic fruit juice.

SINGLE-BARREL Rested or aged tequila bottled from one barrel, as opposed to the typical blending of multiple barrels. The term does not appear in the Norm and is not regulated by the CRT.

SPIRIT Distilled alcoholic beverage. A "hard liquor."

SPIRIT CATEGORY Type of spirit, defined by sugar source, production method, or regional tradition. The Distilled Spirits Council of the United States recognizes the following global spirit categories: American whiskey, brandy/Cognac, Canadian whisky, cordials/liqueurs, gin, rye whiskey, Irish whiskey, rum, Scotch, tequila/mezcal, and vodka.

SUPERIOR ALCOHOLS *Alcoholes superiores*; also called "higher alcohols." Alcohols with more than two carbon atoms. They are regulated by the Norm.

SUPER-PREMIUM Used as a marketing term with no regulated definition. The Distilled Spirits Council of the United States uses "super-premium" as a price category. In 2022, super-premium tequilas were those retailing for around $40 to $50 per 750 ml bottle in retail stores.

TAHONA Stone wheel, generally weighing about two metric tons. A traditional method for extracting aguamiel.

TAILS Liquid condensed and collected toward the end of distillation, after the second "cut" has been made.

TAHONA

TAPATÍO/TAPATÍA As a noun, a person from Jalisco, especially Guadalajara. Also used as an adjective to describe any noun.

TAVERNA In Jalisco, a rustic distillery.

TEQUILA Spirit distilled from the hydrolyzed, fermented sap of the blue agave within Mexico's DOT region, under the auspices of the CRT. Also the municipality in Mexico's Jalisco state, for which the spirit is named.

TEQUILA VALLEY The *valles* region of Jalisco west of Guadalajara, birthplace of the tequila tradition. The primary tequila-producing towns of "the Valley" are Tequila, Amatitán, El Arenal, and Magdalena.

TEQUILENSE A person or thing from Tequila.

TEQUILERO/TEQUILERA A person who makes tequila, or a person or thing associated with tequila.

TERROIR The concept that a specific natural and cultural environment imbues a food or beverage with distinct flavor characteristics.

TEQUILERO

VINAZAS "Stillage" or "vinasse." Liquid waste from the tequila-making process.

VINO "Wine." Traditional term for liquor, including tequila, in Jalisco.

YEAST Single-celled fungi that convert sugar to alcohol in the fermentation process.

Selected Bibliography

Bowen, Sarah. *Divided Spirits: Tequila, Mezcal, and the Politics of Production*. Oakland: University of California Press, 2015.

Gaytán, Marie Sarita. *¡Tequila!: Distilling the Spirit of Mexico*. Stanford: Stanford University Press, 2014.

Gentry, Howard Scott. *Agaves of Continental North America*. Tucson: University of Arizona Press, 1982.

Gschaedler Mathis, Anne C., Benjamín Rodríguez Garay, Rogelio Prado Ramírez, and José Luís Flores Montaño, eds. *Ciencia y tecnología del tequila: Avances y perspectivas (2a edición)*. Guadalajara: CIATEJ, 2015.

Hutson, Lucinda. *¡Viva Tequila! Cocktails, Cooking, and Other Agave Adventures*. Austin: University of Texas Press, 2013.

Luna Zamora, Rogelio. *La historia del tequila, de sus regiones y sus hombres*. Mexico City: CONACULTA, 1991.

Machuca, Paulina. *El vino de cocos en la Nueva España: Historia de una transculturación en el siglo XVII*. Zamora: El Colegio de Michoacán, 2018.

Navarro, Alberto. *Larousse del Tequila*. Mexico City: Larousse, 2016.

Valenzuela Zapata, Ana G., and Alejandro Macías Macías. *La Indicación Geográfica Tequila: Lecciones de la primera denominación de origen mexicana*. Mexico City: CONABIO, 2014.

Valenzuela Zapata, Ana G., and Gary Paul Nabhan. *Tequila: A Natural and Cultural History*. Tucson: University of Arizona Press, 2003.

Vera Cortés, José Luís, and Rodolfo Fernández, eds. *Aguas de las verdes matas: Tequila y mezcal*. Mexico City: Artes de México y el Mundo S.A. de C.V. / INAH, 2015.

Resources

Pennsylvania
Tequilas
1602 Locust St.
Philadelphia
tequilasphilly.com

Texas
Suerte
1800 E. Sixth St.
Austin
suerteatx.com

Las Almas Rotas
3615 Parry Ave.
Dallas
lasalmasrotas.com

Esquire Tavern
155 E. Commerce St.
San Antonio
esquiretavern-sa.com

Washington
Agave Cocina
100 Republican St.,
  Ste. 100
Seattle
agavecocina.com

Barrio
1420 12th Ave.
Seattle
barriorestaurant.com

Mission Cantina
2325 California Ave. SW
Seattle
missioncantinaseattle
  .com

Poquitos
1000 E. Pike St.
Seattle
vivapoquitos.com

Washington DC
Oyamel Cocina Mexicana
401 Seventh St. NW
oyamel.com

Wisconsin
BelAir Cantina
1935 N. Water Street
Milwaukee
belaircantina.com

MEXICO
Tequila tours
Experience Agave
experienceagave.com

Mexico Tequila Tours
mexico-tequila-tours
  .negocio.site

Mundo Cuervo
mundocuervo.com

Casa Sauza
casasauza.com

La Cofradía
tequilacofradia.com.mx

Tequila bars
La Tequila
Avenida México 2830
Guadalajara
latequila.mx

El Gallo Altanero
Calle Marsella 126
Guadalajara
galloaltanero.com.mx

Matilde Mi Amor
Calle Colonias 221
Guadalajara
matildemiamor.com

Farmacia Rita Pérez
Calle Colonias 79
Guadalajara

De la O Cantina
Calle Argentina 70
Guadalajara

El Tasting Room
Panamá 134
Puerto Vallarta
eltastingroom.mx

CANADA
Tequila bars
La Mezcalería
1622 Commercial Drive
Vancouver, BC
lamezcaleria.ca

UNITED KINGDOM
Mail-order tequila sales
Casa Agave
casa-agave.com

Tequila bars
Cafe Pacifico
5 Langley St.
London
cafe-pacifico.com

Mestizo
103 Hampstead Rd.
London
mestizomx.com

El Bandito
41b Slater St.
Liverpool
elbandito.co.uk

El Cartel
15-16 Teviot Pl.
Edinburgh
elcartelmexicana.co.uk

Dos Dedos
Edgar Mews, Bartlett St.
Bath
dosdedos.co.uk

Ojo Rojo
106 Commercial Rd.
Bournemouth
ojo-rojo.co.uk

La Pantera
5 Quay St.
Cardiff
lapantera.co.uk

Crazy Pedros Bridge
 Street
55-57 Bridge St.
Manchester
crazypedros.co.uk

Southside Tequila Joint
447-449 Wilmslow Rd.
Manchester
tequilajoint.com

400 Rabbits
15-16 Hurts Yard
Nottingham
fourhundredrabbits.co.uk

Piña
3 Harvest Lane
Sheffield
barpina.co.uk

AUSTRALIA

Mail-order tequila sales
Top Shelf Tequila
topshelftequila.com.au

Tequila bars
Bodega Underground
55 Little Bourke St.
Melbourne
bodegaunderground
 .com.au

Méjico
Melbourne and Sidney
mejico.com.au

Los Amantes
339 Victoria St.
Brunswick
losamantes.com.au

Loquita
17 Garema Pl.
Canberra
loquita.com.au

Pepe's Newmarket
184 Enoggera Rd.
Newmarket
pepesmexican.com.au/
 pepes-newmarket

Tío's Cervecería
4-14 Foster St.
Surry Hills

Acknowledgments

Thanks to everyone at Artisan, especially Judy Pray for the green light and Bella Lemos for the professionalism, patience, and guidance that greatly improved this book and my writing. Thanks to my agent, Jud Laghi, for finding the ideal publisher.

I am immensely grateful to the dozens of tequileros and other experts whom I interviewed for this book. To everyone profiled in these pages and to the many more behind the scenes, thank you.

This book provided a delightful pretext to collaborate with my dear friends Grover Sanschagrin and Andrés Morán Gutiérrez. I am honored by their contributions and by their years of friendship and camaraderie.

As a first-time author, I benefited significantly from collegial advice about publishing from Ronda Brulotte, Ted Genoways, Jacob Grier, and McCormick Templeman.

I am lucky to have some extremely eloquent and erudite friends, several of whom generously provided critical feedback on many drafts of this book. Nico Azios, Tracie Cone, C. Flink, Don Heiser, Kami Kenna, Alejandro Nuñez, Felisa Rosa Rogers, and Scarlet Sanschagrin—I am in your debt, sincerely.

For sharing their scientific and technical expertise, I am grateful to Nico Azios, Danae Cabrera Toledo, Emilio Ferreira Ruíz, Hendrik Giersiepen, Kami Kenna, Rocío Rodríguez Torres, Leopoldo Solís Tinoco, and Óscar Vásquez Camarena. For historical insights, to María de Jesús Arambula Limón, Ted Genoways, Germán González Gorrochotegui, María Cristina Hernández Garrido, Luís Margáin Sainz, and Jorge Rivera Landeros. And to Greg Cohen, Jake Lustig, and Devlin McGill for observations and data on the US tequila market. Needless to say, any errors, omissions, or *tonterías* are solely mine.

My formal tasting studies have included valuable instruction from David Yan González, Jaime Villalobos Díaz, Ana Maria Romero Mena, and Franz Hajnal. *Gracias, maestros.*

My understanding of tequila and Tequila has been enriched in innumerable ways by David González Castañeda, Mickaël Thomassin, Margarita Arana Cisneros, Francisco Cerrillos Hernández and the whole Cerrillos family, Aracely Álvarez Gómez, Liliana Barrera Velázquez, René Carranza Torres, Maricruz Castro Lamas, Sonia Espínola de la Llave, Claudia Gómez Cortés, Martha Gómez Ramírez, Rodolfo Gómez Delgado, Óscar and Mario Hernández González, Carlos Hernández Ramos, Alfredo and Antoñio Landeros Sandoval, Leobardo "Piña" Padilla Miranda, Marisol Sevilla Bañuelos, Tetsu Shady, and Grisel Vargas García.

I wrote this book amid challenging and uncertain circumstances: lockdown, quarantine, an international move, and the first year of a doctoral program. Through all that and more, Felisa Rosa Rogers has been a keen but compassionate critic of my writing and the greatest source of joy in my life. Felisa, this book would exist without you, but it wouldn't be nearly as good. And neither would I. Thank you.

Index

CLAYTON J. SZCZECH is a writer and sociologist who has been studying and teaching about Mexican alcoholic beverages since 2006. He has operated the groundbreaking educational tour company Experience Agave since 2008. He cofounded La Cata, the first brand-independent tasting room in Tequila, Jalisco, in 2016. He has been featured in the *Wall Street Journal*, *Los Angeles Times*, *Sunset*, *The Guardian*, *AFAR*, *Wine Enthusiast*, *Virtuoso Life*, on CNN en Español, and on Amazon's *Distilling Mexico*. He holds numerous certifications related to tequila and mezcal, is a permanent legal resident of Mexico, and is currently pursuing a doctorate at the University of Utah. His academic work focuses on the socioeconomic and environmental outcomes of Geographical Indication regimes, with an emphasis on Mexico. In 2023, he was selected as a National Science Foundation Graduate Research Fellow. *A Field Guide to Tequila* is his first book.